When My Mother Is Most Beautiful

★

Rebecca Suzuki's *When My Mother Is Most Beautiful* is a tender love letter, a cosmology of identity, and a bouquet of elegiac questions across time and space. Woven with matrilineal care, I loved how this collection fused poetry, prose, and radical translation under one glimmering moon.

—Jane Wong, author of *Meet Me Tonight in Atlantic City*

With a poet's precision and a warrior's heart, Suzuki weaves a searing story of intergenerational loss and longing through her pages, wielding translation, footnotes, and landscape to forge beauty out of destruction. The poems in this book play with unanswerable questions about home, identity, belonging, and love, and we watch Suzuki break her own heart over and over again while building a world out of language where mothers become gingko trees and there are rabbits inside the moon.

—Kelly McMasters, author of *The Leaving Season: A Memoir in Essays*

In Rebecca Suzuki's *When My Mother Is Most Beautiful*, the author charges her readers to remember that those lost still echo in the living—whether familial mythology, ancestors, or language. The spell of the bilingual writing in Japanese and English writing systems illustrates how one interrupts the other, asking for the deferral of meaning to summon from beyond the page, the spirit of the reader's understanding. Neither world is complete for Suzuki's speakers without each another. This book casts its magic through rigorous hybridity of form and genre, inventing itself as the reader plods deeper and deeper into Suzuki's affective reservoir. This entire book is a marvel, a summoning, a moon song in the night just when I needed it.

—Rajiv Mohabir, Author of *CUTLISH* (Four Way Books 2021),
ANTIMAN (Winner of the 2021 Restless Books Prize for New Immigrant Writing)
and translator of *I Even Regret Night: Holi Songs of Demerara* (Kaya Press 2019)

Rebecca Suzuki's book, *When My Mother Is Most Beautiful* is one long searing narrative ode to the speaker's mother, a mother the speaker both connects to and one she disconnects from. The gentle declaratives are both arresting and coy, as images barrel across the page. Ultimately, this gorgeous book tries to answer, but cannot, the question related to family, country, race, history: "How long are we made to contemplate our belonging?"

—Victoria Chang, author of *The Trees Witness Everything*

For her memoir *When My Mother Is Most Beautiful*, Rebecca Suzuki mixes prose, poetry, drama, translation, haibun (a form that combines prose and haiku) to create a gorgeous hybrid and multivocal collection where even a footnote can read like flash prose. A few lines in "An Interaction at a [Convenience Store]" reveals how readers will be offered numerous reading experiences: inside the English text, there is Japanese in Japanese, Japanese romanized, and available footnotes. For me, because I understand some Japanese, there are times when I grasp the meaning and immediately become a participant in the scene. More often, I can't read the Japanese and I feel bewildered. Other readers may feel unsure or curious. And afterall, such responses are salutary. It is good for a book to elicit strong feelings. Whatever one's reading experience, Suzuki's powerful debut collection is as intimate as one's breath.

—Kimiko Hahn, author of *Foreign Bodies*

★

When My Mother Is Most Beautiful

Rebecca Suzuki

Hanging Loose Press,
Brooklyn, New York

This book is the winner of the annual Loose Translations Prize, jointly sponsored by Hanging Loose Press and the graduate writing program of Queens College, City University of New York. The competition is open to students and recent graduates of the MFA translation program.

www.hangingloosepress.com

Printed in the United States of America 10 9 8 7 6 5 4 3 2 1

Hanging Loose thanks the Literature Program of the New York State Council on the Arts for a grant in support of the publication of this book.

Cover art by Ryan Fark
Book design by Nanako Inoue
Authors' photo: Camila Hernández Solano

ISBN 978-1-934909-77-5

For my mother and sister

CONTENTS

1.
Face Forward

Moukohan

When I was 産まれた[1]
my mother traced
over the bluish bruise
spot on my back
Mongolian Spot[2].

Was she checking
for common ancestry despite
having just birthed me
the umbilical cord sliced
right in front of her?

Was she feeling
energy from all
who were alive before me
before us, our only marker
this bluish hue that
eventually disappears
from our backs[3]?

As my mother traces
my 蒙古斑
does she see burial grounds
of all who have passed?

Does she see in the blue
a moon, a spot in the sky
proving our existence
eventually disappeared?

---

1. born
2. モンゴリアンスポット: 蒙古斑
3. Mongolian blue spots, now referred to as dermal melanocytosis, are a kind of
   temporary birthmark caused by a collection of melanocytes in the deeper layers
   of the skin. 80% of Asian, 80 – 85% of Native American, 90% Polynesian and
   Micronesian, 46% Latin American and 90-96% African American infants are
   born with this birthmark. It is a marker of non-European descent.

桜

When I was born, my mother wanted to give me a Japanese name: 桜 (Sakura), which means cherry blossom, but when she proposed this idea to her sister, she discouraged my mother saying, "桜 is beautiful, but it withers and dies in just a week[4]," and that is the difference between my mother and my aunt.

---

4. 桜は一週間で散ってしまうから桜って名前はつけないほうがいいよ

Other Side

There are two sides to every story:

My mother wanted to name me after the most important symbol in Japanese culture. A source of longing, of worship, of happiness. A beauty to uphold, to respect, to celebrate. A symbol of spring, of renewal, of hope.

My aunt wanted to prevent my name from being a reminder that life is fleeting. That it is very short. That beauty doesn't last, and mortality always wins. A symbol of termination, of falling back into the ground.

There is a third side to this story: by the time it came to choosing a name for me, their mother had been diagnosed with a terminal illness.

おばあさん[5]/ おばあちゃん[6]

My おばあちゃん died before she was really considered おばあさ
ん by society.

She had three grandchildren, but still worked every day in the
greenhouses across the street from her house until she got sick, the
greenhouses she'd built with her husband, my grandfather, where
they grew exotic plants. My grandfather died years before my おばあ
ちゃん, leaving her to do all of the work alone.

My おばあちゃん was diagnosed with lung cancer right after I
was born. Not enough protection from the harsh chemicals used
in the greenhouses. That's probably how my grandfather also
got cancer so young. Before the disease spread, she held me like
treasure and walked all around the neighborhood, showing everyone
she knew her third grandchild. "She was so proud of you," my
mother likes to tell me. "She said you were going to be special."

When my おばあちゃん became too sick to leave the hospital,
she covered the walls of her room with photos of her grandchildren.
She would look at them when it was too painful to do anything else.
I don't know who took them down when she died. I don't know who
kept the photos. Are they in a box somewhere in the house she used
to live in, which is now my aunt's house? Were they cremated with
her body? Did the hospital staff get rid of them?

I wish my おばあちゃん had lived long enough for me to be able
to call her my おばあちゃん.

---

5. Obaasan: 1. Grandmother; 2. Old woman; female senior citizen.
I struggle with finding an equivalent in English. Calling someone
"grandmother" and "old woman" in English is rude, but it's quite
endearing in Japanese. This is probably because of the way the West
views old age and the elderly vs. the East. In the West, older people
are seen frequently as a burden, and it is common for families to put
aging members in a nursing home. As a country, the U.S. doesn't seem

to care for the old. See: https://www.aarp.org/caregiving/health/info-2020/covid-19-nursing-homes-an-american-tragedy.html. Yet in the East, where Confucianism has had a significant influence, older people are highly respected and taken care of. Putting one's aging parents in a nursing home is still considered taboo, and society seems to prioritize their wellbeing. See: https://theconversation.com/social-care-japanese-style-what-we-can-learn-from-the-worlds-oldest-population-96936

6. Obaachan: Grandma. An even more endearing and informal version of おばあさん. Maybe something similar to Granny or Nanna. What I would've called my grandmother if she were still alive.

Spirits are other beings, they are not you

My grandmother, grandfather, and many other dead relatives visit us as spirits during お盆[7] each year, for four days in mid-August. My aunt prepares big meals to offer to the spirits and we say things to each other like, "Hey, I see おばあちゃん sitting behind you, say hello!" I feel so comforted knowing that my ancestors, most of whom I couldn't meet in this life, are with me.

On the last day of お盆, my aunt makes a horse out of a thin cucumber or eggplant by sticking disposable chopsticks into them as legs. We all walk to the beach with the horse. When we get there, we light incense and let the eggplant horse float away in the water. That is how the spirits travel back to heaven.

There is one rule when we send our ancestors back: *whatever you do, do not look back*. The whole way home, we must keep looking straight ahead and never turn back to look at the beach. This is so that our ancestors don't see our faces and become tempted to follow us back home instead of going back to 天国[8].

As a child, I understood it as an act of love for the ghosts: If I really love them, I will not turn back because 天国 is better than staying on earth as invisible spirits.

Now, I see it as an act of self-love, too. We miss the dead, we want those who left us to come back, but we must not keep looking back at their death. We have to keep going, face forward. Live. With the promise that their spirits will come again next year.

---

7. Obon: festival of the dead. It's a nationally celebrated holiday in Japan, where families visit their 実家 (jikka, the home they grew up in) and spend quality time together. The town celebrates with summer festivals where people gather to dance 盆踊り(bon-odori), eat food from food stalls, and play carnival games like 輪投げ (wanage, ring toss) and 金魚すくい (kingyo sukui, goldfish-catching). Since Obon is in mid-August,

my sister and I were often in Japan to celebrate it. It was my favorite holiday. Our aunt would dress us up in our cousins' yukatas and we would spend the evening eating 焼きそば (yakisoba), たこ焼き (takoya-ki), candied apples, and cotton candy from the food stalls. Swinging from our wrists would be goldfish swimming in a bag bloated with water. When it was time for fireworks, we would find a place to sit on a patch of grass and stare at the night sky.

8. Tengoku: paradise; heaven; afterlife

2.
Permanent Non-Erasable Trail

桜 *as Mother*

My mother has had the same phone for over six years, and because she is taking a trip to Japan next month to attend a middle school reunion where she will see her classmates from over 40 years ago, and she doesn't want to be seen with her outdated iPhone SE encased in a browning, ripping wallet case, she gets a new phone. She was on the fence about the trip for a while, but I told her more than once, "It's been 45 years since you've seen most of these people, you have to go!" To me, it seemed like more than a simple reunion: a return. Or a reclaiming of something

"I have to change my background photo. The year of the tiger is over," my mother mutters while playing around with her new phone. For the past year, her background has been the photo of a tiger made of lanterns she took last January, when we went to visit my sister in North Carolina and we all went to a lantern festival.

It is now the year of the rabbit, and I ask her teasingly: "Will you change it to a photo of a rabbit?" and she says "そうだね..." while looking through her camera roll, not bothering to look at me. Later, she calls me over to show me what she has chosen. She puts the phone very close to her face and her finger swipes up theatrically to open the phone she's not used to. おおお[9]—she has been making this sound since Brian the Verizon guy set up her new lavender iPhone 14 and placed it onto her palm like an uncooked egg.

I see that my mother has chosen of course, a photo of 桜. I am not surprised. It is a beautiful photo she took last year or maybe a couple of years ago, of night-time 桜. The blossoms shine white under a bright streetlight in front of the backdrop of a dark navy sky. Underneath the tree in the distance is the tiny New York City skyline, twinkling in rainbow. The tree is billowing above the city, as though mothering it.

---

9. Ōo

Permanent Non-Erasable Trail

Every new year
my mother
insists on writing resolution
in black bold calligraphy.
Every new year
she spills a bit of 墨
in the ink tray and watches it flow
forwards and backwards
as she moves the inkstick
up and down
time passing and memory pulling back.
When the 墨 is dark enough
She dips brush in pool
gets rid of excess
and follows the brush
with her hand
make a permanent
non-erasable trail.
She sits in 正座[10]
on a western dining room chair
which she mended
after the cat tore it up.
Her back is pin-straight
her face relaxed
eyes determined
other hand placed neatly
on the lower left corner.
The resolution is generic
something like "fortune" or
青空—blue sky
but with the 墨 she traces
her memories until
she is in her 習字[11] class
writing in the same posture
waiting for her mother
to pick her up.

10. Seiza: kneeling with the tops of the feet flat on the floor, and sitting on the soles.

11. Shuuji: penmanship; calligraphy. Many children take 習字 lessons in Japan.

before before before

My mother took up horseback riding as a hobby when she was young, before she had me, before she met my father, before she moved to England, before before before. I remember as kids my sister and I would play with the riding whip and heavy horseshoe our mother kept from those days. My mother loves horses—says they are smart and gentle and playful and loving and she finds joy in the way they gently sweep up a carrot from her palm with their soft snout. Horseback riding was a hobby of my mother's that didn't last very long, but long enough for her mother to always buy extra carrots at the grocery store and to gift her riding boots.

When my mother left for England, her horseback riding days came to an abrupt end. She left her riding boots in her room and said goodbye to her mother, who was constantly reminded of her absence because of the tall, chocolate leather boots that sat in the corner of the room. My grandmother had never left the country. My mother was the first one in the family to fly in an airplane.

When my mother came back with a foreign lover, my grandmother told her, "I didn't raise you to marry an American!"

As soon as I was born, my grandmother's anger dissipated. She saw in me both: American and Japanese. And how peacefully I slept, even when the two parts of myself were supposed to be fighting.

My mother never took up horseback riding after she came back from England. Too busy with motherhood, with work, with survival. Too expensive. I imagine her though, before her husband died, before her mother died, before she had me, before she met my father, before she moved to England, before before before when she had long, silky black hair that would fly behind her as she rode her horse in the chocolate leather riding boots gifted to her by her mother.

a mother's beauty

My mother says that she regrets many things she said to her mother.

My mother says that there are things she only understood about her mother when she became a mother herself. But it was too late at that point. She was already gone.

My mother had to watch her mother die not long after giving me life.

When my mother and I pass by ginkgo trees, either in the summer when their fan-shaped leaves are green or in the fall when they are yellow and begin covering the ground below like carpet, my mother likes to tell me that only some of the trees make 銀杏[12]. She notes that she hardly ever sees 銀杏 on American ginkgo trees and wonders why.

It is only the female ginkgo trees that produce 銀杏, though they need sperm from the male trees to produce them. The nuts have a pungent smell—some describe it as dog poop, others as vomit, and others as stinky cheese. Whatever its comparison, the smell is noticeable and this is probably the reason we hardly see any 銀杏 on our walks. A friend tells me that he's seen female ginkgo trees being chopped down in the middle of the night. He tells me also of a female tree with a hole drilled through it, kept alive by the two male trees next to her. A dying female tree, forcibly kept alive by the male trees that cannot stop producing pollen.

Ginkgo belongs to the Ginkgoales order, which appeared over 270 million years ago. Ginkgoes are descended from trees that used to feed and shelter dinosaurs. Six ginkgo trees are known to have survived the atomic bombing in Hiroshima.

My mother tells me that her mother loved 銀杏. She loved it so much, in fact, that one time, she ate too many. It's unclear how many she ate, but afterwards, she felt nauseous and had a nosebleed.

To cook 銀杏, you have to first put a crack in its tough whitish outer shell and slowly roast it on a pan. Once roasted and peeled from both its outer shell and thin inner shell, the nut is light green like a peeled grape, somewhere between the color of a ginkgo leaf in the summer and a ginkgo leaf in the fall. When you bite into the gummy-like nut, you initially taste its slight sweetness or bitterness, but are then hit with a burst of umami comparable to the shock of biting into a piece of Camembert. I've only tried it a few times—the ones sitting at the bottom of chawanmushi, and I'm still getting used to its punch.

You are not supposed to eat more than 10 銀杏 at once because the nut can cause gingko toxin poisoning. Its symptoms include: stomachache, nausea, vomiting, nervous irritability, convulsions, and sometimes death. This means my grandmother was poisoned, at least a little bit.

My mother says that her mother got the nosebleed from the 銀杏 because they're *too* good for you. *Too* filled with nutrients. The body doesn't know how to handle it.

When I pass ginkgo trees I think: this is the perfect tree.

When I pass ginkgo trees I think: be careful with beauty.

---

12. Ginnan: gingko nut

桃色 *in the sky*

My friends in Japan have started posting photographs of 桜 on Instagram. They've bloomed very early this year, it's not even April yet.

Because 桜 signifies renewal and they usually bloom in April, the school year in Japan begins in April. I remember being welcomed by a sea of blossoms when I walked to elementary school for the first time. My mother and I wore matching rose blouses that she'd made just for that day, and I carried my brand new pink ランドセル (randoseru) that my aunt bought for me. Back when I started elementary school, all the girls carried red ランドセル and the boys had black ランドセル. They sold other colors like pink and blue and yellow, but nobody really bought those. My aunt took us to the mall to buy my ランドセル as a celebration of becoming an elementary school student. I was going to pick the red one, but my mother stopped me. "Be different," she said. I wonder if I listened and went with the pink because I knew that I was already different. Red didn't belong to me. I was already not like the other Japanese kids. Or maybe I wanted to be different. Maybe categories and boxes already bothered me. Fortunately, this custom of girls having red ランドセル and boys having black ランドセル has been phased out. Now, girls and boys are free to choose whatever color they like, and if you walk into an elementary school now, you'd see children carrying a rainbow of ランドセル.

A part of me is filled with joy when I see the photos of the 桜— what a wonderful feeling to have friends who are able to enjoy the beauty of cherry blossoms, especially after what happened a few years ago, when they bloomed and fell amidst human panic. But a part of me is filled with a longing I know will not be fulfilled. A jealousy that will not settle. It makes me feel desolate. I show my mother a photo, and I can tell she shares my feelings. Her initial reaction is a smile, a sigh and a "きれいだね〜!" but then it's wiped off, replaced by an emptiness, an unfulfillment.

She told me the other day that she didn't know how many more times she'd be able to see the 桜 bloom before she died. She's 60 now, which is older than the age her mother died, and they only bloom once a year.

I don't know what she thinks of when she looks up at the 桃色[13] in the sky:

her gone mother
her gone father
her gone lover
the smells of her childhood home
rain pattering on the roof
the sleeping faces of her infant daughters, now ~~gone~~ grown
time passing
her gone mother
taste of white rice grains on her tongue
clinks of glasses filled with 酒 in the 居酒屋 of her early twenties days
death
the warmth of her grandmother's hand
soft grass tickling her bare arms
sand between her toes and her lover's soft hair
her favorite pair of shoes
smoke trailing from a stick of incense
her gone mother

But these are just my guesses.

---

13. Momoiro: peach color. The skin of a Japanese peach is soft pink. I have thought deeply about the color of 桜. I've translated it into the English word, "pink" in the past, but the word ピンク (pinku) has entered Japanese vocabulary, and ピンク is a brighter, flashier shade of pink than 桃色 is. The pink of a cherry blossom petal is not loud—it evokes a gentler, more peaceful feeling

when my mother is most beautiful

Every morning when I was three before my sister was born, my mother and I walked to my preschool together. Along the way we'd pass houses, trees and trees and trees, shrubs, and a little pond with large lotus leaves growing out of it. Always after a night of rain my mother would stop and tilt one of the giant leaves to show me the droplets of water chasing each other on its smooth, wide surface. When the droplets came too close to the edge, my mother would tilt the leaf back so they wouldn't fall, saying おーとっと！[14] I would watch, mesmerized, squealing when the droplet came close to falling into the green pond below, never to be a single droplet of water again. お玉杓子さんみたいだね—like tadpoles, my mother would say, her smile illuminated by the slow-waking sun, still low in the sky. During those few minutes, I would forget all about having to go to preschool, about having to say goodbye to my mother. I cried every single morning when she turned to walk toward the door. Nothing else mattered though, when she was rolling around water droplets on a giant leaf to make them look like tadpoles. "Here, you try!" she'd say, waiting for me to hold the sides of the leaf and let me navigate the little marbles on an endless surface of green.

---

14. Ōottotto!

Dear マミー[15],

How did it feel for you when people used to question your motherhood after looking at you, then at me, then back at you? How did you hold back the anger when they asked you questions like, "本当にあんたの子なの？全然似てないね。[16]" What about that time some woman walked up to me, a two-year-old and asked, "この人あんたのお母さんなの？[17]" I asked you how you responded, and you said you brushed her off, but how did you do it without losing your cool? How dare strangers question your motherhood. How dare they make assumptions just by looking. Were they blind to all the love you poured into me, or the love I had for you? Couldn't they see how devoted you were to me, giving me every part of you for me to selfishly consume?

Remember how angry you were with me once, because you told me that you are 人[18] and I refused to believe you. I said, "マミーは人じゃないよ[19]" and you became furious because you thought that I didn't see you as a human being. But the truth is, I saw you as so much more than a human being. I'd understood 人 as a person—any person. But to me, you were my mother. You were so much more than a person, how could I reduce you to a 人? A single word? I didn't know how to articulate all that though, and I remember tearfully accepting your scolding: "Okay, I understand now. You are 人." But truthfully, I didn't see you as 人 until recently. That you are also a human being. But you are still so much more. I still don't know what to do with all of that—do you ever notice?

I don't think anyone questions it anymore. You being my mother, I mean. I have your eyes, your eyebrows, your cheeks, your birthmark on my nose, your smile, your beating heart.

リベッカより

---

15. Mamii: most Japanese children call their mothers ママ (mama) or お母さん (okāsan) but I've always called my mother マミー (mommy).

16. "Is she really your child? She looks nothing like you."

17. "Is this your mother?"

18. Hito: 1. man; person 2. Human being; mankind; people 3. Human (Homo sapiens); humans as a species; 4. Character; personality 5. Man of talent; true man 6. Another person; other people; others 7. Adult. It is a hieroglyphic character resembling a man standing sideways (with his legs apart)

19. "Mommy is not a person."

3.
Remember that We are Plants

neck support

When I try to heal myself from pain, I become idle and stuck like I'm living inside a bottle of glue.

When my body is wrecked with a heavy stone first falling on top of me and then somehow entering me, for me to carry at the bottom of my stomach, I feel so heavy and stay far from everywhere.

I don't want to do.

This morning, I dragged my body to the bathroom to wash myself and to brush my teeth, and in the time that I spent, staring at the sad in my eyes, my mother placed a single flower in a water-filled glass bottle and put it on my desk.

I'd seen the same flower earlier in a big vase, in a family of flowers sitting on top of the dining table as I had my breakfast. Her neck was bending from the weight of her heavy petals and I'd asked myself: "Does she know how I feel?"

But my mother had healed her—given her neck support: the first motherly instinct.

My mother says one thing to me when I notice the flower in my room: 花は咲く[20].

My mother is the only person who knows how I've been all my life.

---

20. Hana wa saku: Flowers bloom / will bloom

remember that we are plants

I tell a friend about my sadness, about my mother's response to my sadness, about the neck support, about the 花は咲くand she tells me: "Remember that we are plants Rebecca."

But am I a plant? Am I a flower, who is chopped off by the root, stuck into a pool of water, and continues to thrive anyway?

Am I a tree, who must grow and root no matter where they are, withstand wind and time, and continues to thrive anyway?

Am I a vine, who clings onto the wall and gets longer and stronger despite the rain, gravity, birds, and bugs, and continues to thrive anyway?

What if I am swept up into a small whistling whirlwind? Can I survive?

I have a conversation with another friend about the fragility of the human species. About how dependent we are.

"I hate being human," he says.
"Let's be trees instead," I suggest.
"We can't. We don't know how to photosynthesize."

Remember that we are not plants.

longing for trees

I always thought that longing for trees was a specifically Japanese feeling. 日本人[21] wait patiently every year for the cherry blossoms to unleash their beauty. To sprout those fragile flowers that fill the air with sweetness. When they finally bloom, 日本人 sit under trees and worship them. Have picnics with them, sing songs to them, laugh with them. But maybe it's not just 日本人. Maybe everyone longs for trees.

During the worst of the pandemic, the only appropriate and guiltless "activity" we could partake in seemed to be going out for walks. My then-boyfriend and I went on a 6-mile walk one time. Originally, we had a destination: a bookstore with a café in it. Our plan was to briefly browse through the bookstore and get a coffee to-go to continue with our walk back, but when we got there, the bookstore was closed except for pick-up and the café had a tiny window into which you could whisper your order. We half expected this to happen but reacted as children do when they don't get what they want. We said, "I don't feel like coffee anymore. Let's just forget it and keep walking."

So, we walked on, all the way to Druid Hill Park and eventually onto a hilly but wide trail with tall trees surrounding us. Around that time, one of my friends was working on a beautiful piece about tree envy[22]. About how humans envy trees because trees have established roots, while we float through life oftentimes without digging into the ground. We care about things that in the end don't matter, while trees stay grounded and committed and beautiful their entire lives. Reading her piece felt profound. Like I'd dug up an old treasure.

As I looked up at the trees on the trail, I longed for their freedom. Growing toward the sky, exploring deeper with their roots, sprouting buds, swaying and sharing secrets with the wind. I thought trees weren't free because they are grounded in place. But they are always moving with the world they are a part of. And sometimes, I feel like even though I am able to move freely on this planet, I am moving in the wrong direction. Against the movement of everyone and everything else.

I don't know if in this moment I long to be a tree or for a tree. A longing implies unfulfillment and sometimes I don't even know what's missing. But the thing is trees don't long for anything. They just are. And I know that's what I am truly longing for. To not long for anything. To just be.

---

21. Nihonjin: Japanese people

22. Which eventually became a chapbook: *Forestwish* by Francesca Hyatt

she's being dramatic as usual

Cousins, aunt, uncle, sister, mother, me
we walk in silence
beach on our backs
leaving waves smacking on concrete
behind

Will the eggplant horse make it
all the way to heaven?

I worry, always the anxious one, but keep my head straight
follow my own feet
I wonder: What would happen if I turned around?"
will I see the tears of my grandmother
the long fingers of my grandfather
keep your head straight
follow your feet

if I ask my family they will all say
"She's being dramatic as usual"
but what if
the eggplant horse washes back ashore
and my ancestors never make it over
and they never find us
what if
they get lost in the ocean
what if
we just all forget

am I the only one
who worries?

Should we have at least watched
the eggplant horse for a little while longer?

"She's being dramatic as usual"

do not turn around
follow your feet
trust the ocean

you'll see them again
next year

whose wish is it anyway?

I think about the time my sister told her teacher at preschool that she wanted to write, "カエルになれますように[23]" on the 短冊[24] one 七夕[25] when she was three or four years old, but instead her teacher wrote, "カエルのような面白い子になれますように[26]."

When my mother went to pick her up from preschool that day, her teacher told her what my sister had said. And how the teacher had "helped" my sister edit the wish a little bit. My mother thought the story was hilarious.

When the story got told to me, I asked my little sister, "本当にカエルになりたいの？なんでカエルなの？[27]" and she said, simply, "うん！カエルが好きだもん。[28]"

And why aren't we allowed to wish to be something that we simply like? Why did the teacher have to change it? The teacher told my mom, "カエルになってしまったら困りますもんねえ[29]" but we all know these wishes are for fun, don't we? If we didn't know that, I would've written the same wish every year: "I wish my dad would come back to me." But I didn't. Because I knew not to take these wishes or any wish, seriously.

What we're allowed to wish for in this world confuses me. And why we wish for things to begin with also confuses me. Are these wishes for ourselves, or are they really for other people?

---

23. I wish to become a frog.

24. Tanzaku: long, narrow strip of paper on which poems are written (vertically) or in this case, wishes for 七夕 are written (also vertically). The paper is usually thin and colorful, with a small hole punctured at the top for a string to be pulled through, so that you can put up your wish on a bamboo branch. When we moved to the U.S., we had to

improvise a bit and write our wishes on regular paper cut into strips and put our wishes on a random plant around the house or one year, on the small fence that surrounded the staircase into our apartment.

25. Tanabata: Star Festival. It originates from the Chinese Qixi Festival. 七夕celebrates the meeting of the deities 織り姫Orihhime and 彦星 Hikoboshi (represented by the stars Vega and Altair respectively). According to the legend of 七夕, the Milky Way separates these lovers, and they are only allowed to meet once a year on the seventh day of the seventh lunar month of the lunisolar calendar. In Japan, it is celebrated on the 7th of July. It is also said in Japan that just as the wishes of these literal star-crossed lovers are met on this evening, so will the wishes of everyone who writes it out on 短冊and hangs them for the night sky.

26. I wish to become as fun-loving as a frog

27. Do you really want to become a frog? Why a frog?

28. Yeah! Because I like frogs

29. We wouldn't want her to become a frog, would we?

4.

My American Father in the Streets of Japan

A gift from my father

After agreeing with my father that their child should have my mother's last name and an American first name, my mother came up with a few possibilities: "What about Laura? Or I really like the name Jillian," she said, standing in a phone booth lit by a single fluorescent lightbulb.

"Well, those aren't Jewish names. We have to give our baby a Jewish name," my father said, standing by the wall in the kitchen of his mother's house in Canarsie, the one that always smelled like bone broth because his mother liked to make soup. He was already dressed in his cab-driving clothes, ready to go to work as soon as they hung up.

"What are Jewish names?" my mother asked, because she'd never met a Jewish person in her life before she met my father.

My mother's mother was unhappy with her—angry even, after finding out that her baby's father was American. "Didn't I tell you about all those times the Americans would drop bombs on us? We'd have to hide underground and then an earthquake would come and we thought we'd be buried alive!" she said to my mother, who listened in silence.

"I've always liked the names Rebecca and Isabella for a girl. What do you think?" my father asked. His mother too, was disappointed in him for divorcing his wife in England and now having a child with a woman in Japan. She often wondered where things had gone wrong.

"I think Isabella sounds いじわる！" my mother said, giggling.

"What is ijiwaru?" He was always asking her how to pronounce sounds, letters, words in Japanese. He desperately wanted to unlock the Japanese language, to mold the foreign into the familiar. He studied it every night, sounding out the words that felt like a jigsaw in his mouth.

"Um… Not nice! No good," my mother said. This was when she still spoke very little English and had limited vocabulary. "Oh, and Rebecca starts with the letter R, right? Like Rie?"

"Yes, it does. Are we decided on Rebecca then, if it's a girl?"

"Yes, Rebecca..." my mother said, stroking her rounding belly...

*   *   *

"What if you'd just named me Jillian? What do you think would've happened? I think it might be a cooler name than Rebecca, to be honest." I said to my mother once.

"I don't think you would've been the same person."

"Do you really think that?"

"べーちゃん[30]はべーちゃんだからね。あんたのお父さんがきめてくれた名前だからね。[31]"

And she thinks, *thank god I didn't choose your name, thank god your father lives in your name, thank god he was able to give you* something, *thank god your father was able to give me* everything.

---

30. Bēchan: What my mother has always called me. I don't think she has ever called me Rebecca. Bēchan comes from my nickname, Becky, which is what my father always called me.

31. Bēchan's Bēchan! It's the name your father chose for you.

in one version of this poem we swim toward life

Holding tightly onto my father's freckled back
warm ocean water like a bath
suspended
in
depth endless

In one version of this poem
we swim
toward life
until sand grazes his stomach
we stand
bare feet on soft earth
he takes my hand
and we walk,
the beach on our backs.

In the actual version of this poem
I let go, let my fingers slip off
he falls into
deep sea that eventually meets sky
alone
while I float toward the surface
alone
water pushing me up and up
My gasp and scream muffled
only bubbles of oxygen
escaping mouth
and waves
spit me up to the sandbar
I wash up
tangled in seaweed
kelp with little seashells
gelatinous legs of jellyfish
and green sea glass
from a broken bottle
its sharp edges dulled

in this poem my father buys me みたらし団子[32]

みたらし団子 is my ダディー[33].
That is to say
みたらし団子 invites memories
of my dead father.
He'd plop me on the back seat
of his bicycle and pedal,
the みたらし団子 shop
his destination.
Sometimes he went down the hill too fast
my hair flying behind me
my hands gripping at the handles until
my knuckles were white
but I'd look at my father's back—safety
and loosen the grip just a little bit.
At the shop, the old women
spun and spun the sticks of 団子
smiling at our visit once again
あーお客さんまたきてくれたのね。今日は何本？[34]
handing us each a stick with the sauce dripping slowly
and I ate the rice cakes like a 子供[35]
(biting from the side and not from the top)
because I was a 子供
I was *his* 子供
sweet sticky sauce all over my cheeks
my ダディー wiping it gently away with tissue
wet with his spit.
In search of みたらし団子
I look everywhere
but I can only find traces
of their smell
in the streets
of Japan
traces of
my American father
in the streets
of Japan

32. Mitarashi dango: I have yet to find good mitarashi dango in the U.S. One day during pandemic lockdown, my mother and I decided to make it together. We mixed 上新粉 (jyoushinko, rice flour) and 白玉粉 (shiratamako, refined rice flour) with warm water, then kneaded the dough until it became the texture of an earlobe. Next, we shaped them into perfect little balls—white and smooth, before poking a wooden stick through them—three to four balls per stick. We grilled them right over the stove in our apartment, the kitchen window letting the smoke out into the building's shared backyard. We then dipped them in the sweet soy sauce glaze. They weren't quite the dango from Japan but still they were tasty.

33. Dadii: what I used to call my father

34. Ah, you've come again my dears. How many sticks will you have today?

35. Kodomo: child

5.

it was gorgeous before you arrived

We followed you, sun

with the Boeing 757 or 737 or whatever those giant planes
are called, as we flew and flew and flew across a bed of blue,
shimmering like forbidden gems, convincing us that the world is
beautiful—at least from above it is, and somewhere on that bed of
blue language shifted and all of a sudden the world I thought I knew,
the 海 and 空 and 太陽 took themselves apart, one stroke at a time
dissipating into the air somewhere—where did they go, the strokes?
I couldn't follow them because Boeings are too fast and we were
in a rush to get to New York City even though I never wanted to go
to New York City. You, the sun, 太陽, you didn't go anywhere—I
followed you, my eyes narrowing, tiring from the brightness, but I
would've disappeared if I stopped looking at you, so I kept my eyes
on you and you said: "I will be here no matter what. The strokes of
your letters are gone, but I am not. Call me by whatever name you
choose." And so I did, I trusted you, even though you hurt me—you
hurt my eyes, and when our tired grumbling plane finally touched
down on the smooth gray tarmac of JFK, you were gone—the
brightness replaced by a blanket of black outside the tiny window,
and inside the cylinder where we all shared the same oxygen for
over fourteen hours, I could no longer breathe, and I remembered
what you had told me, and I called out to 太陽 but nobody answered,
and so I said louder, 太陽! *Taiyo!* Which is gibberish in English,
and somebody hushed me from somewhere inside and I was told to
just close my eyes and relax and accept this dark, silent space.

it was gorgeous before you arrived

It rained for the first few days in America, the sky filled with billowing gray clouds releasing their water on us. "It will clear up soon, it was gorgeous before you arrived," our family told my mother, even though she had bigger concerns than the bad weather. I don't remember anything aside from the first night, when my mother, sister and I were surrounded by family who had gathered at my grandmother's house to welcome us as we sat huddled on her couch, and also the rain and the wet, the unfamiliar air and water sticking to my body too soon. But on the fourth evening it finally stopped raining and the skies cleared and before the three of us piled on top of my aunt's air mattress, we made sure to look up at the night sky and there was nothing there but the moon, so spectacular, so quiet, so delicious, my mother pointed to it and said, ほら、ぼた餅みたいで美味しそうだね[36] and I saw some of those strokes I thought had disappeared come back together to form familiar shapes in the sky, the moon turning into ぼた餅 just like the offering my aunt would sometimes make to my ancestors living somewhere between the ocean and sky.

---

36. Hora, botamochi mitaide oishisoudane: look, it looks delicious like botamochi.

floating

There's a photo of me in an album somewhere, smiling down from the top of a tree in my early days in America. We settled first in Bayside, Queens, a walking-distance from Crocheron Park, filled with trees and grass and squirrels.

In the photo it's early summer, which means it's before I started summer camp at the YMCA and before I walked into an American public-school classroom for the first time since my very brief half-year as a kindergartener in Brooklyn. In the photo I am wearing one of the few outfits I brought over from Japan—an oversized pink T-shirt with my favorite cartoon character, Tweety Bird peeking out of a tiny pocket on the right side of my chest and its matching Tweety shorts. Dangling on my feet are brown slippers my mother bought for me at Payless. My short, middle-parted hair is tied up. I am smiling with teeth and dimples.

I used to want to climb trees all the time when we first moved to America. I didn't want to share the dirt path with dog walkers and runners and pedestrians and my mother and my sister—I wanted to climb up a rough, thick, sturdy trunk, scooch over carefully on a long, resilient branch and claim my seat, closer to the sky, closer to home, hovering above unfamiliar, unrootable ground.

early days

It is May, it is one of our first weeks in America, it is one of our first times exploring Brooklyn on our own: my mother, my sister, me. Maybe a trip to the welfare office. Or a doctor's office. Or searching for an apartment. I can't remember why we were there.

My mother has a daughter on each side of her, holding tightly onto their hands so she doesn't lose them. When we try to fool around by skipping or hopping, she tells us to やめなさい！and tugs at our hands.

「マミーのおでこにいつもシワがよってるよね。[37]」my six-year-old sister whispers to me. 「そうだね。いつも怒ってるね。[38]」

We are all hungry, and I announce that I want to eat pizza. I have a fading memory of the pizzeria in Brooklyn my father once owned very briefly before the business closed. I want to try it again, after all these years, even though my father and his pizzeria are both gone.

「おかしいなあ、この辺にあったよねえ、ピザ屋さん。[39]」my mother wonders out loud, scratching the side of her chin.

「ねえねえ、ピザ持ったトマトのおじさんさっきいたよ！[40]」my sister says.

「何言ってるの？[41]」my mother says, brushing it off as six-year-old nonsense.

「何、トマトのおじさんって？[42]」I say, the hunger making me more irritable.

「だってみたもん！ピザ持ってたよ、トマトのおじさん！[43]」my sister is also insistent.

We wander around in circles. We see the same bodega at least three times on the street corner but there is no pizzeria to be found.

「トマトのおじさんあっちだよ。[44]」my sister says.

「じゃあ、あっち行ってみよっか。[45]」my mother finally resigns.

So, we follow the tiny feet of my baby sister, dodging the crowds of people on the sidewalk even though it's a weekday afternoon, and she directs us straight to Tomato-Man holding a tray of pizza. She didn't mention that it was just a silly statue in front of a pizzeria instead of an actual living tomato-man holding a pizza, but she wasn't lying.

We enter the shop and into the aroma of sweet tomato sauce, cheese, garlic, and oregano. I immediately spot the refrigerator stocked to the brim with bottles of drinks.

I half expect my father, a skinny Jewish man with a dark beard to pop out from the back. What comes out instead are pies and slices—out of the oven, piping hot, cheese oozing off the side with hot orange oil pooling at the top.

We get our slices, sit down, and take the first bite: a little bit of burnt crust, sweet and tangy tomato sauce, savory, stretchy mozzarella cheese. We all sit in silence in the hard, plastic booth, biting and munching and tasting and swallowing and reaching for the lone bottle of Seven-Up in the middle of the table. This is no pizza or experience you could get in Japan.

「ねえねえおねえちゃん！今、マミーのおでこにしわよってないね。[46]」 my sister points out.

I look and she's right. My mother's forehead is smooth. She is even smiling a little. She looks almost like us—a kid.

「おでこ、ピカピカだね！[47]」 I joke, and my sister giggles in the way only six-year-olds can giggle. 「ピカピカ、ピカチュウ！[48]」 she yells out, and enters her world of colors and imaginary characters.

I return to my pizza, back to the slice waiting on a paper plate. When I pick it up it warms my hand and the smell invites me to bring it closer and closer to my face until my mouth can no longer resist and with the utmost urgency I chomp and chew, chomp and chew… And I glance outside the smoggy, dirty windows and see him—the Tomato Man holding a tray of pizza, forever smiling, forever enticing New Yorkers to stop by and have his pizza.

---

37. Mommy's forehead always has wrinkles.

38. That's true, she's always angry.

39. How weird, we passed by a pizza shop around here, didn't we?

40. I saw a Tomato-Man holding a pizza.

41. What are you talking about?

42. What the heck is a Tomato-Man?

43. But I saw him! And he was holding a pizza, the Tomato-Man!

44. The Tomato-Man is that way.

45. Okay, let's try going that way.

46. Hey onēchan, mommy's forehead doesn't have wrinkles now.

47. Her forehead's shiny!

48. Pika pika (onomatopoeia for shiny in Japanese), Pikachu!

貧乏ゆすり[49]

Why does the phrase 貧乏ゆすり mention 貧乏? Poor. What does that have to do with leg-shaking?

Poor people would shake their legs out of nervousness.

Is this just another jab at poor people? Why is making fun of the poor so normalized and accepted? Where is the nurture?

Did I also shake my legs when:
we first moved here and my mother could barely afford a place to live in a city like New York and we had to go to the welfare office and we had to go grocery shopping on buses running on Sunday schedules and we had to roll our dirty laundry on shopping carts and we had to take a bus and a subway and a bus to the doctor's office that took government insurance and I was the only fourth grader who bought nothing at the Scholastic Book Fair and my sister and I could pick just one snack for the week because food stamps had a limit and on birthdays we made our own cakes and my sister and I made collages as gifts for our mom using old photographs and newspaper cutouts and my sister and I would fight over the TV on Saturday mornings because the local channels would show two cable-TV shows at the same time and...?

Is that the reason I still shake now, because I don't really know how to shake the poorness out of my body?

The way it felt,
to feel judged all the time, to feel less than, to feel insignificant? Is that the source of the fear and the shake? Maybe I still haven't been able to quite shake it off (PUN INTENDED)

Did my wishes to have it better crash with others' wishes? Was my wish too weak, too small?

Do I still have 貧乏ゆすり because according to the world,
monetary richness is the only determinant of a successful life?

Poor people would shake their legs out of nervousness.

---

49. Binbou yusuri: shaking one's legs (usu. Unconsciously); tapping
one's foot; fidgeting one's legs. Literally translated, the phrase
means "poor person's shake." Other than giving this word a
negative connotation because it's considered ill-mannered, why
would poorness be associated with shaking one's legs? I dug into
its etymology a little bit. Its origins could be rooted in five different
possibilities: 1. Because the act looks like a poor person shivering in
the cold; 2. It was common for poor people to shake their legs when
an usurer appeared to collect money; 3. During the Edo Period, it
was said that if you shook your legs, the god of poverty would pos-
sess you; 4. The shaking looks similar to a poor person moving and
working all the time, according to those in the upper class; 5. Poor
people would shake their legs out of nervousness.

a haibun about fleeting friendships

Every evening after 9pm when calls were free for T-Mobile users, you would call me and I would lie on my bed so I could talk to you. We were in sixth grade and best friends; we both had single mothers.

You asked me once during lunch, "Do you know what FUBU stands for?" I was wearing a FUBU sweatshirt without knowing anything. My mother liked to take me to Daffy's, the discounted department store near Penn Station, and I'd wear whatever she bought me there. I was eating 焼きそば[50] my mother had stir-fried that morning; you were eating school lunch: heated up ravioli from a can on a Styrofoam tray that MS158[51] served that day. "It stands for 'For Us By Us.' For people like *us*."

You called at 9:07 that evening and towards the end of the conversation I said I was sorry.

"Sorry for what?"

"For the sweatshirt."

"Oh, it's all right, you didn't know."

"I won't wear it again."

"Doesn't mean you can't wear it, I just want you to know what it stands for. Did you know Tommy Hilfiger said he doesn't want Black people wearing his clothes?"

I never wore FUBU after that. You said it was okay, but I knew what it felt like for people to steal something that belongs to you and claim it as their own. Or laugh at it.

In music class we sat next to each other and I told you that in Japanese your name, Tori, means bird, 鳥 and your face lit up like I'd shown you an actual bird.

After sixth grade, we both stopped taking music class and you started sitting at a different table during lunch. Maybe you got sick of having to explain everything to me. Maybe you were tired of my ignorance. Maybe you were just bored by me. Nine o'clock would come and go without your call.

Now we're just friends on Instagram—I see you've changed the spelling of your name from "Tori" to "Tauri" and have a little girl named Lynx. A lynx with a bird for a mother—how beautiful.

I still sometimes think, maybe at nine you'd call me again, "For old time's sake" and you'd tell me everything that happened in high school then college then after college and you'd tell me about your daughter and your mother, but my phone screen stays blank.

The silence after a phone call
Pause, a tangible closure—an act of ending
when you're most alone

---

50. Yakisoba: stir fried noodles usually with vegetables and meat

51. Marie Curie Middle School 158, located in Bayside, Queens. A magnet school and the motto is, "Together, we create success!"

The Three of Us Still Talk About This Moment and It's Still Funny

It is 2003. We are all at Penn Station
my mother, sister, and I
waiting for the LIRR to go home
but we are hungry.

We scan the food shops
spot a McDonald's, a pizza shop, Subway, KFC
and I immediately remember the TV ad
for popcorn chicken from KFC
(thank you, America).

"Mommy can we try the popcorn chicken?"
She says okay and we walk over
to the old, mustached man, Colonel Sanders beaming,
the restaurant is a bucket of fried chicken.

In line I point to the menu
glowing above the cashiers' heads
"A medium popcorn chicken, ok?"
My mother nods deeply, wallet in hand.

When it's our turn my mother looks up,
gets confused by all the alphabet and pictures
chicken bucket, tender bucket, pot pie, fries
and I remind her, "Popcorn chicken!"

And she snaps back into her body, swallows,
"An order of medium pa..pa…papapapa chicken!"
Sometimes English is a heavy gate in her mouth
now, it is tiny, rolling raisins.

The cashier smiles, understands anyway
and puts in our order
and while we wait, we are all clutching our stomachs
doubled over in laughter.

"Did you hear that??
Papapapa chicken!!"
My sister and I are without mercy
cruel, even

but our mother joins us in our laughter
we are all clutching our bellies
and we reap in our reward:
our papapapa chicken.

6.
美味しい団子はアメリカにない

A Scene From a Play Called *Sunset at Shinmaiko*

Setting: Shinmaiko Beach. On the concrete steps that lead down to the water. It is December 31, 1999. R is 8; J is 4; MOTHER is 37. The sun is setting, dipping into the far ocean, bleeding into the sky in pink and orange and purple.

MOTHER (holding up a 1991 camcorder, recording): Okay girls, we have to start saying goodbye to the sun and to the 20th century.

R and J wave both arms, facing the sun and away from the camera.

R: BYEEEEE おひさまー[52]!! BYEEE 20th CENTURY!!!

J: BYEEEEE おひさまー!! BYEEE 20TH CENTURY!!!

MOTHER: R, why don't you show me your tricks on the jump rope?

R picks up jump rope from the ground and starts jumping and doing tricks, like swinging the rope twice around on a single jump, or crisscrossing arms. She is talented.

J imitates R's movements with an imaginary jump rope.

MOTHER moves the camera slowly from one to the other.

MOTHER: Okay, let's eat the cup ramen before it gets dark.

R&J (together): YAY YAY!

MOTHER puts the recorder down and takes out NISSHIN Cup Ramen and a thermos from her bag. She pours the hot water into the cup ramen and places it on the ground. Steam rises slowly out of the Styrofoam cup. She covers the top with the paper lid and places unbroken disposable wooden chopsticks on top. She picks up the camcorder again and presses the record button.

MOTHER: R, what's your wish for the new century?

R: I want to learn more tricks on my jump rope!

MOTHER: J, what's your wish for the new century?

J: I want more stuffed animals!

MOTHER chuckles

MOTHER silently records R&J hopping around, randomly bumping into each other or hugging each other, laughing. Being children.

MOTHER puts the recorder down, picks up the cup ramen and slowly peels back the lid all the way. She breaks the disposable wooden chopsticks.

MOTHER: Okay, let's eat!

R&J: YAY!

The three of them sit down, facing the water. The sun is halfway swallowed by the ocean. The orange and red sky makes MOTHER nostalgic and R & J excited. MOTHER blows on the surface of the noodles and passes it to R. After a few slurps, R passes it to J. After J has had some, she passes it back to MOTHER. They keep passing it around until all the noodles are gone and there is a little bit of soup left.

MOTHER: Can I finish it?

R & J Nod.

MOTHER slurps loudly and sighs after she is finished.

MOTHER: Wowww, isn't the sunset beautiful?

R: Uh huh!

MOTHER: We're going to have the BEST new century!

R&J: Yeah!!

-end scene-

---

52. Ohisama: what children sometimes call the sun. It is both endearing and respectful. Paints the sun as godlike.

our memories into a heap of other endless memories

Back in Japan, we had a 軽自動車[53] like many other households. She was a gray box with no seatbelts in the back, and she would rumble down the road towards the grocery store or to my Saturday violin classes. Her name was Michelle #2, because I used to name every car my mother owned Michelle. Michelle #2 was a manual, so sometimes, she would pause for a second before climbing up a hill, changing gears and sighing in her passive aggressive ways.

On good days, our Kei felt fast and smooth, but on bad days, she would leak things out of her tail and stop in the middle of the highway. That happened twice.

This is a memory with our Kei car. One of the last ones, before she was driven for the last time to a car junkyard and taken apart and crushed into the ground.

It's our final week in Japan. I am nine years old, and it's late March, so the weather is just beginning to warm up again. People are anticipating the cherry blossoms, but it's probably not going to happen until right before we leave. My mother has somehow loaded the car with our couch. My favorite couch. I'd sat on it every day since we moved back to Japan when I was four or five. It usually had a cover with bears on it, but in the car, it sits naked and without pillows. So exposed.

My mother tells my sister and me to sit on the couch during the drive because the backseats are folded over. We are ecstatic at such an exciting ride, and we sit next to each other giggling. As our Kei crawls slowly onto the highway, my six-year-old sister and I wave through the back window to the cars behind us. The drivers who notice give us friendly smiles and occasional waves back.

But beyond the waving; beyond the giggling; beyond the sideways ride, I am saying over and over in my mind, "Goodbye couch." I know it's the last time I'll ever sit on it; the last time my sister will ever sit on it; the last time anyone will ever sit on it. I want to protest and say "No! Let's not throw the couch away!" but how could we bring this to America? It's just not possible.

Our Kei groans and sighs all the way to the junkyard, complaining about the extra weight. When we get there, robotic workmen in light gray jumpsuits run over and carry the couch away without ceremony. I watch them take our memories into a heap of other endless memories.

My mother fixes the backseats and we all climb back into the Kei. She has to turn the key a few times before the engine starts. Maybe the Kei knew she was also soon going to be turned into a heap of memory.

---

53 Kei jidosha: Also known as a Kei car or K-car, it is a Japanese category of small vehicles, including passenger cars, vans, and pickup trucks. Kei cars are designed to comply with Japanese government tax and insurance regulations, and in most rural areas are exempted from the requirement to certify that adequate parking is available for the vehicle. This especially advantaged class of cars was developed to promote popular motorization in the post war era. Kei cars would not pass inspection in the U.S., which is the reason we do not see them here.

美味しい団子ってアメリカにないことない？[54]

The last time I was in Japan was on New Year's in 2019 with my sister. Our aunt fed us sushi and crab hot pot and fried shrimp and oysters and ぜんざい[55] and やきもち[56] and おせち料理[57] and 団子 from my favorite place with the green wrapping[58] because our aunt has always spoiled us.

My aunt's house which used to be my grandparents' house looks exactly the same as it has always looked, which is not a good thing because it's so old and in desperate need of repairs. It's cluttered and falling apart and it's never a surprise when a spider the size of a hand makes an appearance on its peeling walls. The house still has a squatting toilet (at least it flushes) but it's down a creepy hallway. My sister used to beg one of our cousins to accompany her and wait for her in front of the toilet door, and I want to make the same request now, but realize I am too old and my cousins probably have better things to do. It is the same hallway and the same toilet my mother used to be scared of when she was a child, growing up in this house.

Every morning and evening my aunt still chants the Buddhist prayer in front of the golden 仏壇[59], beating rhythmically on the 木魚[60] to keep the tempo. At the end of the prayer she sounds the おりん[61] once and starts again. After the third time, she rings the おりん three times to signal the end of prayer.

In the morning my aunt makes an offering for our ancestors in front of the 仏壇: small goblets of cooked rice and some water; unpeeled fruit if there is any; a box of dried snacks someone has brought over to the house as a gift. Our ancestors must eat before us, always. Then every evening, my aunt collects the goblets of rice in a small wooden box and carries it over to the kitchen, to empty into a Tupperware to use for the next day's lunch or to make onigiri. My younger sister used to always ask her for a goblet so she could eat the hardened, cold, day-old rice. She'd eat it like ice cream, taking small bites as though it were a delicacy. My aunt would delight in my sister's strangeness.

When we were younger, we would all pray together: my mother, aunt, sister, cousins, me—the children fighting for the stick to drum the 木魚 with or the one to ring the おりん with. We all knew the Buddhist chant and sang together, sitting in 正座 on cushions on the floor, our feet tucked under our bottoms and our backs pin-straight, our palms kissing in front of our chests as we faced the altar. The framed photos of my grandparents and great-grandparents smiled down on us from above as we prayed. This is the reason I know what my grandparents and great-grandparents looked like. I'd see these big photos every day growing up. When we were done chanting the prayer three times and the おりん was rung, we would all tuck our heads closer to our chests, close our eyes, and pray in silence for a minute or two. I wonder what I used to pray for.

My sister and I left our aunt's house just a few days after New Year's because we wanted to go to Kyoto and Osaka and Kobe. Our trips always feel too short. On the last evening, I listened from the other room as my aunt prayed alone in the altar room. I was secretly hoping for her to suggest that we all go together like the old days, but I suppose she's used to doing it by herself now. I tried to tune out the sound of the television that my cousins were laughing at and listened to the rhythmic drumming, the *makahanyaharamita...* and I couldn't remember the rest. The prayer I'd recited over and over and over again as a child I no longer had. All I could do now was listen from a faraway room hoping that at least the sweet high note of the おりん would travel far enough to transport me back to the days when my family was one.

---

54. Oishii dangotte amerika ni naikoto nai?: Isn't it impossible to find good dango in the U.S.?

55. Zenzai: In this context, the word refers to red bean soup made with azuki beans but the word also means well done!; bravo!

56. My personal opinion is that popularizing mochi ice cream in the U.S. is the worst thing that could've happened to mochi. When I

talk about mochi with my American friends, most of them think it's a casing for ice cream. Or a topping for froyo.やきもち is my favorite way of eating mochi. It's grilled and dipped in a soy sauce-sugar dip and wrapped in seaweed. When you take a bite, the hot mochi stretches like cheese and the soy sauce-soaked seaweed rips satisfactorily with your teeth. It's so simple and so delicious. I also love that やきもちを焼く (grilling mochi) means to be jealous. Like a slow burn maybe? Or because when mochi's being grilled, it stretches and expands like a balloon, sort of like our thoughts when we're jealous? Not quite sure.

57. Osechi Ryōri: Traditional Japanese New Year foods dating back to the Heian Period (794 – 1185). Osechi is composed of many small dishes arranged in special boxes called jūbako. Each dish has a meaning behind it. For example: 黒豆, koromame (blackbean) is a symbol of health; かずのこ, kazunoko (herring roe) is for "many children" over the next year; and 紅白かまぼこ, kouhaku kamaboko (red and white fish cake) is to show love for the country because the colors of the Japanese flag are red and white.

58. 美味しい団子ってアメリカにないことない？

59. Butsudan: Buddhist altar. The altar exists in most Japanese homes, and in my aunt's house, there is an entire room dedicated to it. The altar has doors, but I have never seen them closed. Or does she close them when everyone's out? I can't recall... Inside the altar are incense holders, bells, platforms for offerings, a rather small painting of Buddha on a scroll at the center. All of it is gold and black.

60. Mokugyo: 木 means tree, and 魚 means fish. It is an instrument made from hollowed out wood in the shape of two fish facing each other, met in the middle by a ball of klesha that they are releasing. With each drum on the mokugyo, more klesha leaves one's body. As a child, I thought it looked more like a resting dog than two fish, but apparently, there is significance behind the fish. It is said that a Chinese monk once "discovered" that fish don't sleep, because they never close their eyes. (Of course, we now know fish just sleep with their eyes open...) Because fish need no sleep, the monk assumed that they had achieved enlightenment. So, fish was/ is revered in Buddhism.

61. Orin: a small metallic bowl that is meant to be gently tapped with a stick to make a pleasant, high-pitched ringing sound.

stone in the light

In a hat with a wide rim, アンティ, my aunt, is gently digging the earth with a small shovel to plant seeds for cucumbers, eggplant, peppers, berries. The vegetables and fruits that, when ripened, she will pick and cook and peel for me to eat. "Here, open your mouth," she will say, her thin, wooden chopsticks gently placing a piece of soft, cooked vegetable on my tongue. After sprinkling the tiny seeds, she covers them with the soft soil like a ritual repeated over and over, patting it down with her hands encased in white gloves. I am nearby, making up songs and words, naming things I don't know the names for. Occasionally, I race over to help her sprinkle seeds—on my sweaty palm, pinching them with my fingers and letting them go into the dips of the earth to magically turn into roots, stems, leaves, flowers, fruits, vegetables. おおきくなあれ！[62] I say, a phrase I learned maybe in preschool or from a picture book. After a while I go back to the prancing and world-making and she says ありがとね[63] as I run across the field. She goes back to planting but glances up once in a while to check on me: to make sure I am within her line of sight. She uses the back of her arm to wipe sweat from her forehead, or she waves to let me know she's following me with her eyes. Sometimes, I stand behind and watch her from the back, crouched near the ground, glowing like a stone in the light. And on this stone, I trace endless circles of love before I can't take it anymore and I run up and embrace her from behind.

---

62. Ōkikunare: Grow!

63. Arigatone: Thanks

eggplant

My mother and my aunt schedule a phone call every month to keep some sort of relationship. They were never close, except for the few years following the death of their mother, when they realized they were the only ones left. During those years my mother became a single mother, and my aunt became my second mother.

Sometimes, I would go back to my aunt's house after school instead of going home, because my mother was going to be out. It didn't occur to me until years later that maybe those were the days when my mother was at her therapist's office, trying to grieve and mourn her husband's premature death.

I notice how it's always my mother scheduling the calls with my aunt. I notice how my mother carries the weight of the conversations: asking about the weather there, about a recipe she's curious about, about Japanese TV shows, about a fad in Japan that she heard about recently but wants to verify. I notice how she avoids the topics that lock my aunt away in silence: the half-torn greenhouses their parents used to work in that have since been neglected; the rice fields and land that are still under their father's name; the desperate need of repairs on the century-old house built by their grandparents that my aunt took over, especially because the next big earthquake is imminent. I notice how my mother appears defeated after she hangs up, looking at me with hurt in her eyes but then joking, "How many questions can I ask about their six cats??" I notice how even after I tell my mother, "You know it's okay not to do these phone calls if you don't want to. If it feels worse than not talking to her, you can stop. Or at least talk to her less frequently" she schedules it every month like clockwork, sending a LINE message to my cousin to set it up because my aunt refuses to own a cell phone.

After each phone call, my mother summarizes the talk. Our only lifeline to our hometown. To our family. Even if I know my aunt mostly talked about the responsibility of taking care of so many cats, I am curious. Maybe she will have an update about my cousins. Or about the neighborhood. Or about somebody I have hazy memories of.

"They don't send the eggplant horse out in the ocean anymore," my mother reveals to me, after one of the calls.

"What, why?? We did that every year!"

"Because they don't want to pollute the ocean. It's not something people do anymore, apparently."

"Pollute the ocean? An eggplant?"

"And the chopsticks… Imagine a turtle with a chopstick in its nose!"

I feel guilty. Maybe even devastated. My biggest worry has come true. *How do my ancestors get home?*

And I look out, past my mother, past the window of our apartment on the tall cliff next to the Hudson River, at the red, industrial ship stopped in the middle of the water in front of the low buildings of uptown Manhattan and realize: I am also not home.

lonely

I read in a book that summer in Japan is very lonely. And I wonder if summer in Japan is very lonely because it is after the 桜 have fallen. When the petals have been reabsorbed by the ground underneath, and the 桃色 is replaced by the green of its leaves.

But after moving to America, summer was the only time I could visit Japan.

The first time we visited, I must've been around 12; my sister 9. We took the plane by ourselves because our mother had to work, and we stayed at my aunt's house for around a month.

On the hot evenings when we went to sleep, with the crickets chirping beyond the window screens, I would think to myself: "We're closer than we think. I fly for half a day and I'm already here. Why was I so worried?" Nothing had disappeared while I was gone. Everything had stayed in place, and there was still space for me.

But on the day we went back to the airport to board our flight back to America, the ocean stretched limitlessly and I suddenly became afraid that the space I thought I had was imagined.

We all cried together at the airport. It began with my sister, then me, then my cousins, then even my aunt. We said, "It's okay, we'll see each other next year," but we knew this was just an attempt to reassure us. We knew that these words could be empty, that there was no guarantee we'd see each other the next year. We were just preparing to live without each other again. To be left, dealing with empty space and silence.

I was constantly made to wonder, "But how do you live with your heart in two different places?" At 12, it felt impossible. The only plausible thing to split my body into two.

Now, when I leave Japan, I am not hit with the same sadness. I don't know what that means. Has adulthood blocked some of those emotions? Is my heart not split evenly anymore? Have I accepted the fact that there isn't space in Japan for me anymore? But do I have space in America?

Summer in Japan is very lonely.

An earlier version of this entry appeared in issue 1 of clotheslines, Fall 2022.

but I can just go to Mitsuwa now

A text I send to my mother in the middle of the day: "When I say the word めかぶ [64] what is the first thing you think of?" I send this after reading a story about めかぶ.

I also send this text because my mother, who left Japan on the same day that I did: April 20, 2001, is still very much more Japanese than I am. She was born and raised in Japan, almost exclusively uses Japanese at her Japanese bank job, keeps the Japanese channel on all day, goes on weekly hikes with her Japanese friends, cooks Japanese food, shops at the Japanese grocery store, and has her computer and phone set to Japanese.

Except one time, I asked her if she missed Japan and she said, "No, not particularly. I don't feel like I'm very Japanese anymore." I was shocked and told her to look at the TV, "You always keep the Japanese channel on. Isn't it because you miss Japan?" and she just shrugged and said, "It's because I can't understand shows in English."

To my text she responds with an image she has taken a screenshot of from Google Images. An image of a generic 4-pack めかぶ you can buy at a store. Underneath it she writes, "このめかぶパック (ˆ＿ˆ) [65]" then, "答えになってるかい？[66]"

I think, *I'll bet she misses walking to any grocery store and being able to buy a pack of* めかぶ *whenever she wants. To not have to go to a Japanese grocery store specifically to find it.* But the truth is, I don't think she cares as much as I think she does. I'm putting more weight into it than she does. I've created a sadness and a longing for home that maybe doesn't exist to the extent that I have made it up. She's moved to New Jersey recently and one of the reasons is to be closer to Mitsuwa, the biggest Japanese supermarket on the East Coast. So, if I were to ask her if she missed the convenience of being Japanese in Japan, she'd probably say, "But I can just go to Mitsuwa now."

She says she never felt like she really belonged in Japan. That she didn't like the way Japanese people judged her all the time. That she never felt like she had true freedom there, because she sensed she was different from everyone else. So, despite English still being a struggle after two decades; despite not really having any American friends; despite still feeling uncomfortable in many American social situations, she would maybe choose to be Japanese in America than be Japanese in Japan.

---

64. Mekabu: thick wakame leaves, from near the stalk. I wonder if my family, who were seaweed makers, also picked and made mekabu, or did they just stick to のり(nori)? Mekabu is not dried out like nori is—it's less reliant on the sun.

65. This pack of mekabu (smiley face)

66. Does this answer your question?

The privilege of maybe

Sometimes, you wonder what would've happened if you ordered a different meal at a restaurant, and sometimes, you wonder how your life would've turned out if you'd never left your home country.

Sometimes, my mother likes to ask me, "Are you happy in the end that we moved here?" She makes sure to include the "in the end" because she knows better than any of us how much we struggled when we first got here.

Sometimes, I give her a satisfactory "yes."

Sometimes, I say "I don't know."

My mother seems to think that I wouldn't have been happy in Japan. That I would've never been able to score high enough on the 受験[67] to get into a good high school, let alone a good university, and that even if I had by some miracle gotten high marks, she could not afford to put me through college anyway. There are very few scholarships or financial aid in Japan. Single mothers are expected to work two, three jobs to pay for their children's education.

"Maybe you would've had kids too young," she says. "Maybe you would've worked some meaningless part time job," she says. Maybe. And maybe not.

All of this is true, or it could not be true. There's a possibility I would've excelled in Japan—it's hard to say. All of this is to say, it was never life or death for us. We had a choice. There is a hypothetical life "if I stayed." I was not escaping death by leaving. I was not running from a civil war, or a famine, or a natural disaster, or a tyrannical government. I left for opportunities.

Choice, then, is the ultimate form of privilege. Being able to wonder, "What if I stayed?" Being able to contemplate a "maybe." Yet I sometimes also wonder if I really had a choice. And even if I did, that choice wasn't mine to make—it was my mother's. What does it mean when you had a choice, but it was made by someone else? Are we really supposed to feel content with being able to imagine a parallel life? Sometimes I wish I didn't have a "maybe." I wish I could say, "This was the only way my life was supposed to happen. No other imagined lives." But the "maybe" always lingers besides me like a pesky fly.

---

67. jyuken: entrance exam. For universities, it is administered every year by the National Center for University Admissions. Students begin studying for this exam as early as kindergarten, and because only attending the top-tier colleges guarantee a promising future, many with low scores wait a year to retake it, rather than entering a lower-tiered school. "During the interim, these young adults, known as ronin, will likely study at a cram school. In pre-modern Japanese history, the term ronin referred to master-less samurai who, absent a teacher, lost their social status and were barred from many traditional forms of employment." Because the word ronin itself implies failure, those labeled as such often suffer from depression. https://www.theatlantic.com/education/archive/2018/01/overhauling-japans-high-stakes-university-admission-system/550409/

infinite number of possibilities

Why is it that when I try to imagine the version of my life in which I stayed, I am swept up by a wave and I feel like I am drowning? Like I can't see anything? Come on Rebecca, focus. 日本に住んでたらどうなってたと思う？[68] And I realize—no admit, it's blank because I have chosen to leave it blank. Because I'm scared. Scared to imagine what my life would've been like if I stayed. The infinite number of possibilities. The sheer amount alone is terrifying to try to imagine. I could've been genuinely happy there, who knows. It just would've been different. *Really* different. There are too many moving parts to life. One tiny thing influencing another tiny thing influencing another until bam! Your whole life changes. Maybe that's what I'm really scared of. The randomness of it all. The control-lessness of it all.

---

68. What would it have been like if I stayed in Japan?

A dialogue / an interrogation

Stranger: Which country do you like better, Japan or the United States?

Brain: How can you ask me that? That's like asking, 'Which parent do you like better: your mom or your dad?'

Me: Umm, I'm not sure. I guess the U.S. I've been here longer, and I don't think I could really live in Japan…

Stranger: Oh, why do you feel like you couldn't live in Japan?

Brain: Because they don't want me.

Me: Well you know, they have crazy work ethics and stuff. I could never get used to that. I also can't speak 敬語[69], so it'd be pretty hard to get a job there…

Stranger: Oh wow, so are you happy you moved here?

Brain: It wasn't my choice. Also, define: happy.

Me: Yeah, I mean in the end I guess it all worked out.

Stranger: So you wouldn't consider going back there?

Brain: I'm an outsider there.

Me: I mean, not to live, no. My life is here.

Brain: Your life is here?

Me: Yes. My friends, my family, my job.

Brain: Is that your life?

Me: I don't know…

Stranger: That makes sense. So, you prefer the U.S. then.

Brain: Is this guy stupid?

Me: Um… Yeah, I guess.

Brain: Stop lying.

Me: I'm not lying.

Brain: You're lying.

Me: How am I lying?

Brain: Where do you feel most like yourself?

Me: I don't know.

Brain: Nowhere.

Me: Anywhere.

---

69. Keigo: honorific Japanese used professionally or with strangers or
with elders. Since I left Japan after the third grade, I never learned
it. Even native speakers of Japanese tell me the difficulties of keigo
because of all its nuances and complex vocabulary and sentences.

What does it mean to be a relic?

When my mother visited me in Japan during my yearlong stay there, she insisted on seeing me in a kimono. She had to trade in my 成人式[70] for high school prom and even hand-made my prom dress, but as my mother, she could not give up seeing me in a 着物[71].

We took a trip to Kyoto, and there, my mother found a kimono rental + photography studio. There was a wide selection of kimonos, and my mother suggested a bright yellow one, but I chose an indigo one covered in pink, purple, and pale blue flowers. It was *my* coming-of-age, after all.

I stood in a tatami-sheeted room in an undergarment and a professional came in to dress me. She was so careful and methodical in the way she worked with the layers of thick fabric, and transformed the 帯[72] into a bursting bow on my back. In the mirror I watched her work and was completely entranced. She noticed and chuckled. "It's not as hard as it looks once you've had enough practice." I didn't believe her.

Even though we'd only paid for me to be dressed and have a few photos taken in the studio, the women in the shop encouraged me to walk around Kyoto in the kimono, as long as I didn't go too far. "Just be careful because it's made from pure silk," they warned me gently.

Until I stepped outside of the dressing room in that 着物, I did not know the immense powers that the garment held. As soon as my mother saw me, her eyes glittered. "Wow," she whispered, before she pulled out her phone to take photo after photo.

When I walked around Kyoto, I felt that I'd been turned into a piece of art. Many strangers approached me to admire and photograph the 着物. "Turn around, show me the 帯!" the older Japanese women shouted, taking photos on their large iPads and phones. There was collective admiration for the thousands-of-years-old clothing, made and remade throughout the years but hardly changed. I was a walking relic, a piece of history, Japan's insistence on preserving beauty. Just by wearing the 着

物, I felt like I was a part of the country's history. That it was my own ancestors who had demanded the craft of this clothing, and somehow, through all the tribulations, I had the honor to embody it and show it to the world.

But I think now of what would happen if I wore the same indigo 着物 in my other home country. How would the gaze change? Many would assume I was just wearing a costume. Some may ask for photographs, but would it be to admire the silk and history of the 着物, or would it be for other reasons? Would somebody be offended? Would I become a target? Or maybe people would be indifferent. What would I feel, rather than pride? And it is these questions that make me wonder where my home country is.

---

70. Seijinshiki: coming-of-age ceremony. Celebrated in January of the year you turn 20. Typically, it is celebrated with everyone from your 実家 (jikka) the neighborhood that you grew up in. The ceremony takes place in a hall (maybe a school auditorium?) and usually, you wear a kimono to the event.

71. kimono

72. Obi: sash for the kimono tied around the waist

As though my only marker for being Japanese is my ability to make 味噌汁

Miso soup is a side dish meant to be served in a small bowl and eaten with rice and other side dishes, but to me, 味噌汁[73] is a marker of my identity

First, I chop up the vegetables I'm putting into the 味噌汁 that day. It could be carrot, onion, potato, kabocha, daikon—whatever is lying in the fridge begging to be used before it rots. 味噌汁 is meant to be flexible, never a fixed recipe.

I add the hard vegetables first into the water being heated in a pot. Slide the carrot bits down the blade of the knife. Listen to the daikon splashing into the pool. Shiitake can be added first too, because it makes very good stock. I then shake some powdered dashi into the pot. This is not the way it was made traditionally, of course. My mom likes to tell me of her days as a child, when she was in charge of shaving dried 鰹[74] for 鰹節[75], which in addition to a thick piece of dried kelp is the real base for 味噌汁. But I don't do this because there is powdered dashi now.

Once the dashi is in, I add more vegetables, let it boil, and lower the heat to add the miso paste. I scoop up a generous spoonful and use a small metal strainer to melt it into the hot water. If you add too little of the paste, you get watery soup you can barely taste. If you add too much, it's overwhelming and takes away attention from the other dishes.

They say in Japan that if you can make good 味噌汁, you can make good Japanese food. Or maybe it's just my family who says this. But because 味噌汁 is the foundation of many Japanese meals, it seems accurate enough.

When I'm finished, I ladle the soup into small lacquered bowls and share it over a meal with my mother. I always carefully examine her face when she takes her first sip. She usually slurps it loudly, pauses, and when it's good, lets out an "あ〜。美味しい！[76]"

When it's not so good, all she does is gently tell me what's missing or what isn't working, but whenever I am criticized, I feel like I've failed at being Japanese. As though the tongue I tasted the soup with didn't understand Japanese flavors correctly. As though my tongue has changed too much. As though my only marker for being Japanese is my ability to make 味噌汁 correctly.

As though somehow, by not getting the flavor right, my ancestors will no longer be my ancestors; the land I was birthed in will never take me back; the language that I first spoke will turn into foreign sounds in my throat.

なんでこんなに自分で自分をせめるのかなあ？[77]

---

73. Miso shiru: miso soup. As a Nagoyan, I prefer the more fermented, saltier 赤味噌 (akamiso, red miso) over 白味噌 (shiromiso, white miso), which is what people from Tokyo or Kyoto prefer (generally). I remember feeling personally attacked one time when a friend told me their preference for white miso, that red miso was way too flavorful and overbearing. White miso on the other hand is sweet and refined, according to said friend. At what point does food preference become a personality trait?

74. Katsuo: oceanic bonito. My mother tells me she almost lost parts of her finger on multiple occasions while shaving katsuo. The blade is very sharp, to cut through the rock-hard dried fish. My mother would have to slide the fish across the lid of a wooden box with the blade on it over and over and when she finally had enough shavings to make a pot of miso soup, she'd open the box to take the shavings out. Sometimes, she'd sneak a little bit for the cat.

75. Katsuobushi: dried katsuo shavings used to make stock

76. Aa, oishii: Ah, it's good

77. Nande konnani jibun de jibun wo semeruno kanaa: Why am I so hard on myself?

仕方ないの?

I wonder which parts of my life are 仕方ない[78] and which parts I can control or fix.

I wonder if some things are beyond repair and it's just 仕方ない and I should give up on it.

I had a brief text exchange with my cousin because it was my sister's birthday yesterday. Since my sister doesn't have the LINE app, both of my cousins messaged me to relay the お誕生日おめでとう！message to my sister.

We were all so close back then. My baby albums are filled with my cousins putting me in a toy shopping cart and wheeling me around the house; me wrapped around in a blanket and lying on their small laps; action shots of all of us chasing one another; my cousins clapping next to me as I blow out my birthday candles; all of us sitting around a table concentrated on a board game; standing in front of shrines in Kyoto; standing next to each other in our 浴衣[79] on our way to summer お祭り[80]. But then we moved to America and they stayed.

For the first couple of years, we would call each other every weekend. Mostly us calling them. I missed them too much not to, and I desperately needed some connection to Japan and to home and to family. Those weekend calls eventually became every other weekend calls, then maybe once a month calls, until there were no more calls.

When I went back to Japan for the first time in seven years in 2014 to work there for a year, they welcomed me and we tried to act like all those years of us being apart didn't really happen. But there was no denying all those years happened. The years were felt everywhere. In the silences. In the language barriers. In the completely different life experiences. In the wrinkles on our foreheads. In the corner of our unsure smiles.

Now we only text on birthdays and holidays. I want to keep the conversation going, but I don't know how.

藍ちゃん：じゅーちゃんお誕生日おめでとう！[81] emoji emoji emoji
藍ちゃん：sticker with lots of hearts
Me: ありがとう[82] emoji emoji
Me: ジュディも２６歳だって〜[83] emoji
藍ちゃん：じゅーが２６歳 emoji emoji みんなで一緒にお祝いするの？[84] emoji
Me: 今日は仕事だったみたいだけど明日家に帰って来るよ！[85] emoji
藍ちゃん：そうか emoji emoji メロンちゃんも来るのかな？[86] emoji emoji
Me: 飛行機で来るからメロンはこれないよ[87] emoji
Me: photo of Melon
藍ちゃん：可愛い〜 emoji emoji 綺麗な猫や[88] emoji emoji
藍ちゃん：また写真見せてな〜[89] emoji

Is it 仕方ない that our conversation has come to this?

---

78. Shikatanai: 1. There's no (other) way; 2. Cannot be helped; unavoidable; inevitable; (there's) nothing one can do; having no choice; 3. It's no use (doing); pointless; useless; no good; insufficient; not enough; 4. Hopeless (person); annoying; troublesome; awful; 5. Cannot stand it; unbearable; cannot help (doing, feeling); dying (to do). The first memory I have with the phrase 仕方ない is when I was picked up from preschool one day by my mother and younger sister who was around 2 at the time, and my mother broke the news to me: "I'm sorry to tell you but your sister ate all of your Christmas candy." For Christmas we had both gotten a little red Santa boot filled with tiny bags of candy and snacks: gummies, potato chips, chocolate, a small box of gum. I was eating the snacks slowly over time so they would last longer. My mother said, "仕方ないでしょ, she's only 2" and that was the end of the conversation.

79. Yukata: light cotton kimono worn in the summer

80. Omatsuri: festival

81. Happy birthday, Juu-chan!

82. Thank you

83. Judi's already 26!

84. Juu's 26! Are you all going to celebrate together?

85. She had to work today but is coming back home tomorrow!

86. I see. Is Melon coming?

87. She's flying, so she can't bring Melon

88. Soo cute! What a beautiful cat

89. Send me pictures again sometime

Is Home in My Hair?

A question to myself: Why is it that I only let Japanese people cut my hair?

Context: I have lived in the U.S. for the past twenty-two years (I am 31) minus the one year I spent working in Japan when I was 22-23. Yet, I have only gone to an American hair salon maybe five times in total.

Proposed answer(s): It just happens to be this way. When I first arrived in the U.S., my mother cut my hair. Then she took me to Super Cuts. Then she found a Japanese hairdresser in Astoria who worked out of her apartment, her gentle black Labrador sitting nearby as she worked on each of us: my sister first, then me, then my mother. We went to her for a few years until she decided to move back to her hometown in Kyoto. Then, my mother heard about Hisako Salon, a Japanese hair salon in midtown, so I went there for the first time when I was 18. And that's where I've been going ever since, except for that one time I went to Hayato Salon, which is another Japanese hair salon on 23rd. I find getting my hair cut to be one of the most intimate experiences. And I seem to only trust a Japanese person to cut my hair, and now I am wondering what this says about me. Do I trust Japanese people more? Do I think that Americans wouldn't know what to do with my Japanese hair? Do I feel more connected to my Japanese side when I go to a Japanese hair salon, where they speak to me in Japanese? Do I view my body as being more Japanese than my mind? These aren't answers, just more questions.

Note(s): I think about the year and a half I spent in Japan working as an English teacher, how my hair grew longer and longer and more and more unmanageable, but I was too scared to call an unfamiliar salon and schedule an appointment in Japanese. I kept putting it off, always keeping my hair in a bun, until a friend and coworker asked if I wanted to go with her to the salon she goes to. I jumped at the opportunity and we went one weekend, to the salon in Nagoya. It smelled like lemongrass and the seats were white and they played soft jazz. When the hairstylist asked about length, I told him I wanted to go short: shoulder-length maybe, and he asked if I was sure. "Aren't you letting it grow?" he asked, and I said no, I just hadn't found a salon to go to until now, I'd been wanting to cut my hair for a while, and he smiled and said, okay. As he was snipping away my damaged, tangled locks he asked, "Where are you from?" I told him that I grew up in New York but really I was born and raised near Nagoya and he widened his eyes, paused his hands and said, "Nice, a local!"

Home is a Smell

I was listening to *The Daily*[90] the other day, and they brought in experts to talk about smells, because that's a big topic these days, isn't it, because of COVID-19. The podcast opened with a sweat-inducing anecdote of a woman who almost lit a cabin on fire because she could not smell the gas leaking out of the propane and was about to light a match. Her sister noticed the smell and came to the rescue just before disaster struck, but the woman talked about her experiences with anosmia, or the inability to smell. She said on average, people affected by anosmia are not diagnosed until their teenage years. To me, that seemed impossible. Smell is such an important part of our lives—how could you not know that you cannot smell until you're 14, 15 years old?

In the podcast someone said, "Smell cannot be described." I was shaken when I heard that. It's true. Smells can only be compared to other things: colors, feelings, other smells, memories, adjectives, but can you really, truly put smell into words? And it dawned on me that perhaps trying to describe a smell is like translating. You cannot get to the actual thing, you can only get so close. You can only describe around it by comparing it to other things.

Yakitori sauce. What does that smell like? Here are words that come to my mind: salt, charcoal, grill, meat, smoke, sweet, sizzling, savory, yellow, evaporating alcohol, fermented soy, walking in between tents with fireworks in the sky, men sweating with cloth wrapped around their foreheads. Do you smell it now?

---

90. https://www.nytimes.com/2021/01/31/podcasts/the-daily/coronavi-rus-loss-of-smell-anosmia.html

7.
Where Do I Begin?

名前は変えないで [91]

When my mother was taking her citizenship test, a pledge to be an upstanding citizen of the United States of America, a clean citizen, a model citizen, a quiet citizen, she asked me: "Should I change my name?"

"Change your name? To what?"

"I don't know, something easier to say. Like Leah. Lia. That's similar enough to Rie, isn't it? Most people mispronounce Rie anyway."

I must've been in middle school, I still had so much to understand, but I remember rushing, hurrying to tell her, "名前は変えないで"

\\

Over a decade later, I am sitting in a car with Rie and our friend Yusuke.

They are speaking to each other—I am listening from the back. They have a conversation about the shooting of Asian women in Atlanta.

でもゆうすけさんもサロンで働いてるもんね。
言わないで。怖くなっちゃうから。
名前がひさこサロンだからすぐ日本のサロンだって分かっちゃうよね。
そうだね。名前変えた方がいいのかな？
そうかもねえ。何も知らない人が通っても日本のサロンだとは分からないように。
じゃあ、エミリーサロンとか？

Yusuke, you work at a salon.

Don't remind me-I'll feel uneasy.

With a name like Hisako Salon, it's so easy to tell that it's a Japanese salon.

That's true. Should we change the name?

Maybe. So that a person just passing by can't tell that it's a Japanese salon.

So, something like, "Emily Salon"?

I think about the neon "Asian" of the "Youngs Asian Massage Parlor," the parlor that the gunman entered and opened fire in, burning into my pupils the night before.

The tone of this conversation is not serious. It's light, playful, interjected by chuckles and laughter. Almost a joke. If it isn't a joke how could it be digested?

\\

How long?

How long are we made to contemplate our name?

How long are we made to contemplate our identity?

How long are we made to contemplate our belonging?

How long are we made to contemplate our body?

How long are we made to contemplate our safety?

How long until it all stops being a joke?

I join the conversation late, I say, jokingly, エミリーって誰？Who is Emily? It makes us all laugh, but I am also not laughing: Who the fuck is Emily? The salon already has a name. Already had a name, for a long time. From the time it opened. It's named after the woman who opened it: Hisako. I say, 名前は変えないで. A pathetic plea. By then the conversation has already moved on.

---

91. Don't change your name

My mother stopped taking the subway in 2020

after reading article after article after article about the attacks, the beatings, the murders of Asian people, the ones that looked like the image she'd see in the mirror as she prepared to go out. For a while she'd wear a hat and a mask whenever she went outside—"maybe they wouldn't see that I'm Asian this way," she'd say, like it wasn't really a big deal. Like it was just a minor inconvenience.

"This is totally not okay," I'd say to her, but she'd simply shrug and say, "Well if I don't like it I can go back, right?"

"Back? Back to where?"

"Japan! 日本に帰ればいいんでしょ。[92]"

I feel an urgency. But I can't quite place that urgency. What is the urgency? Or, maybe the question is: where do I begin?

"No, that's not how this works. You are American," I tell her.

"Oh. Am I? I don't know…"

"You are!"

"Okay," she says, before adjusting her hat in the mirror by the door, letting me know she's late.

She looks at me—the bitter American, smiles reassuringly, and waves goodbye.

---

92. I should just go back to Japan, right?

January 24, 2023

The headline reads: "California staggered by deadly back-to-back mass shootings[93]"

What to make of it all. What to do with my body when my mind is bombarded like this. How to stop my mind from trying to make sense out of nonsense. How to accept as reality all the violence.

"The attacks seemed especially baffling in part because the suspects in each were men of retirement age, much older than is typical for perpetrators of deadly mass shootings that have become numbingly routine in the United States."

Typical. Numbingly Routine. United States.

The shootings happened at dance halls as people celebrated Lunar New Year. All of the victims in their 50s, 60s, 70s, enjoying probably, the limited time they dedicate to having fun. Letting go. Being free. The victims whose pictures are released look like my mother, my aunt, my grandmother, my friends' mothers, my friends' aunts, my friends' grandmothers.

I turn to other people when I don't know what to do; what to say.

"Our bodies are not designed to absorb and process this much violence, loss, and grief," says Min Jin Lee.

"I've been encouraged to try and hold both realities, to acknowledge the devastation and fear in the violent realm, while also acknowledging the mundane and delightful moments of the daily realm," says Chanel Miller.

---

93. https://www.reuters.com/world/us/california-staggered-by-deadly-back-to-back-mass-shootings-2023-01-24/

My Greatest Desire

I went to a bar in Brooklyn for a friend's birthday and we listened to a live jazz performance. I couldn't stop staring at the pianist—the passion with which she slammed down at the keys, creating the most delectable sounds that bounced around the walls and found our ears, making unforgettable imprints. She played with her entire body—head bowed, eyes closed, feeling the notes with every cell, swaying and bouncing with the melodies. She played in a kimono—thick red lines like low-glowing embers on black fabric traveling across her body, tied together on her waist with a thick, black and gold obi.

During intermission one of my friends at the table, my Japanese friend, suggested we say hello to her. So, we stepped outside to the courtyard, where the pianist was sitting and resting between sets.

"I just wanted to tell you how amazing you are," I told her.

After she thanked me, I added, "And your kimono. It's so beautiful."

She thanked me again and said, "I wear a kimono every day."

My heart fluttered. I wanted to jump into the seat next to her, to sit close to her and rest my head on her chest and ask her to be my lifelong friend, to take her hand into mine. It was hard to explain why I had this sudden burst of desire.

I found her Instagram account shortly after and in almost all her photos she is wearing a kimono. A deep blue kimono with rectangular patterns; a dotted sky-blue kimono; a purple kimono with white triangles by her knees; a rainbow kimono tied with a yellow obi; another purple kimono with tropical flowers and an obi with a black cat peeping through from the side.

I think about this woman who wears a kimono every single day. To every single performance. Proudly. Effortlessly. Shamelessly. Seamlessly. And plays the piano in all those ways, too. And explains nothing to anybody because she doesn't owe anybody an explanation. And speaks with the music she creates with her hands, body, and mind.

A friend sends me a post on Instagram…

About Gwen Stefani. An interview she did recently about the success of her early-2000s fragrance line, "Harajuku Girls." She mentions her love for Japan in the interview—how exposed she was to the country and culture because her father used to work for Yamaha and would travel back and forth between Japan and the U.S., bringing back with him his observations about the country. When she was finally able to visit Japan, she went to Harajuku and said to herself, "My God, I'm Japanese and I didn't know it." She says this in the interview and adds: "I am, you know. Even though I'm an Italian American – Irish or whatever mutt that I am – that's who I became because those were my people, right?"

Her… People… As in, the people she… (fill in the blank)? Am I reading too much into things?

I respond to my friend with just a single line: "Her *visits* to Japan lmfao" because there is no use dissecting any of it. About how white people with power are always trying to steal parts of my culture they have deemed "cool." About how colonialist it is to say that a country is theirs after a couple of visits. About how fucked up it is to make assumptions and observations about an entire country from the mythological tales your white father brought back from his business trips. About how when you mix different types of white and call it a "mutt" you are still pure, but that's far from the truth as soon as you mix color. About how she appropriated an entire culture for a fragrance line she was profiting from. But there is no use going over any of it with my friend, because she is also Asian American and she gets it and she's tired like I'm tired and all I want to do is scoff, roll my eyes, and laugh because anger takes too much energy.

How we:

Eerie, to read the line, "I still can never be too careful" in a book the day after a mass shooting in Atlanta[94], where eight are left dead, six of them Asian American women.

The first attack took place at "Youngs Asian Massage Parlor." I stare at the photograph of its neon sign, the word "Asian" burning into my pupils.

How we: put so much preparation in facing our world: map, water, emergency food,compass, and yet.

How we: are made to confront a barrel of a gun anyway.

How we: are fed lies; unrealities: "Captain Jay Baker of the Cherokee County Sherriff's Office said during a Wednesday morning press conference the 21-year-old suspect claimed the shootings weren't racially motivated even though six of the eight people killed were of Asian descent."[95]

How we: are given no excuses for stepping out of line. Chinese Exclusion Act. Japanese internment camps. COVID-19.

How we: have been made to conform to a delusional narrative, and yet "the suspect indicated he 'has some issues, potentially sexual addiction,' Cherokee County Sheriff Frank Reynolds said. He saw the spas as a temptation that he wanted to eliminate, Baker said."

How we: are handed a microphone made of a barrel of a gun; the killer is given a platform for his excuse—for what, exactly? (We all know what, though).

How we: sit back, take it back, take it apart.

How we: are made to deal with the constant thought: *People would rather see you die than* be a part of this country.

I am overwhelmed with exhaustion. What do I do? Where do I go?

How we: must learn to move all over again.

94. https://apnews.com/article/georgia-massage-parlor-shooting-8-dead-9e39706c523c733a6d83d9baf4866154

95. https://www.cbsnews.com/news/atlanta-spa-shootings-asian-women-suspect-sexual-addiction/

Scribbles in 蝋石[96]

When we are afraid of going anywhere far because our sisters were just ended with a finger on a trigger, a small pull, just a single moment on this ever-revolving earth, a revolver ending it all. When we'd like to be swallowed by earth, for her to take us back into her womb, not for a phallic weapon directed out of a car window to shoot us dead.

And yet.

When we finally arrive, only to be met with more mouths of phallic guns, what do we do other than scribble on the street with 蝋石?

We scribble, and keep on scribbling:

#StopAsianHate
#HateIsAVirus
#HateHasNoPlace
#WeBelongHere
#NotYourModelMinority
#StopTheHateStopRacism
#EndTheViolenceAgainstAAPI
#DoYouSeeOurPain
#ここが私の居場所
#IAmNotAVirus
#IAmNotYourScapegoat
#WeAreAmericans

---

96. Rouseki: agalmatolite; pagodite; figure stone

depth where oxygen disappears

I've been thinking about centering and decentering a lot lately.

"But why can't he decenter himself for a second and center you, or the both of you instead?" I found myself recording on a voice message to a friend, who was worried that her partner was giving up on their new relationship because he was afraid of it.

Do we think of "centers" and "centering" because the earth is round, and roundness implies a center?

There is talk about centering whiteness and decentering whiteness.

If I write without centering whiteness, am I always writing fiction? Is it always a translation?

Translator Sawako Nakayasu tells us: "Say translation in lively defiance of the social desire to translate like everyone else." She also tells us: "Say the more time I spend writing and translating and making art, the more they all blend into each other. Say the more time I spend being human and knowing and caring about other humans, the more the conventional structures of human relationships blend and regroup and reinvent those structures."

Does a whiteness-not-at-the-center America exist? Or is that just in my hopes and dreams? If it doesn't exist now, can we ever make it there?

\\

A friend sent me an article called, "Inside the Blue Hole[97]," with the subtitle: "On Trump, manatees, and the depths where oxygen disappears." There is this line in the article: "United States, a country founded on the genocide of Indigenous people and the enslavement of Black people, started at the bottom, and thus has little room to sink."

But it seems, time and time again, that we sink. And we are sinking. That the "bottom" is actually endless. That the very idea of a bottom is fallacy. People are starting to see this and lose hope.

Are those already at the center afraid of decentering because decentering implies a toppling? Like a top that stops spinning and loses its center. Is that what people imagine when they imagine themselves decentering? The earth suddenly breaking free from its axis, spinning wildly out of control, flinging people off its surface into endless space.

The closer you are to the center, the less you have to work. The farther away you are from the center, the more distance you have to travel. So, I guess it's also about doing or not doing more work.

What would happen, though, if even for a single day, all of us decided to step out of our centers, the center of our bodies, and decided to center something else? Somebody else? What would happen then? Will the earth really topple? Or would the weight just become evenly distributed and we could finally collectively release a breath—relaxed, composed, still, unmoving.

---

97. https://www.sierraclub.org/sierra/inside-blue-hole-manatee-trump

Do You Like Horses

You should distribute your weight evenly on top of a horse so as not to strain your body or the horse. People forget that horses are also living beings, not machines. Yet there are horses shackled and tied to carriages, like the ones that trot on the concrete of Central Park. Blinders block their view of the world, coachmen pull at the leather straps and sometimes whip them while riders grin, sitting right behind the horse's ass[98].

I think of the horse I saw once, on a bus in Ireland while driving between rolling hills of fresh green grass. How it stood up on its hind legs, thumped back into the ground, shook its head gleefully, and began running as fast as it could across the hill— no destination; no leather straps; no riders. I'd never longed to be a horse until that moment.

I think of the horses[102] on the Great Plains of America, running like the horse in Ireland, the indigenous people letting them be, even though it was the Spaniards who brought them over[99]. "Let them share this land," they must've said[100].

But nobody says that anymore[101].

Please make sure to read the footnotes.

I think of the horses made to run towards their own death as the indigenous people fought against guns to keep their Great Plains free; I think of the heavy bodies crashing down, crashing down, crashing down to the ground, then buried in dust.

And I wonder: How many more bodies will be buried in dust fighting for a home?

I think about how many wars horses were made to fight in, even though it was never, ever their war.

Why do I feel like so many of us are still at war, and more horses are dying? And will die? And left in the dust?

The Ponokomitta promised the protection of humans as long as humans loved them. And they did. The humans who lived in America loved and loved and loved until the settlers came and there was no longer love. There was no longer anything. Where did they go, the Ponomokittas?

They never went anywhere. They were always here. It is language that destroyed and erased the Ponomokittas. They were always here, they are still here. Maybe language can bring them back.

---

98. Many are suspicious of the treatment of these horses that draw carriages around and around Central Park. There has been at least one incident recently in which a horse collapsed in the middle of the road, probably from exhaustion: https://www.cbsnews.com/news/ryder-carriage-horse-died-new-york-city-collapse/

99. This is wrong. According to the dissertation, "The Relationship Between the Indigenous Peoples of the Americas and the Horse: Deconstructing A Eurocentric Myth" by Yvette Running Horse Collin, "Although Western academia admits that the horse originated in the Americas, it claims that the horse became extinct in these continents during the Last Glacial Maximum (between roughly 13,000 and 11,000 years ago). This version of "history" credits Spanish conquistadors and other early European explorers with reintroducing the horse to the Americas and to its Indigenous Peoples. However, many Native Nations state that "they always had the horse" and that they had well established horse cultures long before the arrival of the Spanish. To date, "history" has been written by Western academia to reflect a Eurocentric and colonial paradigm."

100. According to the same dissertation as above, "As Indigenous Elders and individuals shared their traditional knowledge and/or their creation stories, it became clear that their perspective

regarding the "horse" was almost completely different than that of the dominant Western culture. To their ancestors, these "beings" were "sacred relatives," rather than beasts of burden that existed to serve the whims of mankind. Therefore, the meaning of the words that were developed by the Indigenous Peoples of the Americas to address this creature are so different from those utilized by the dominant culture, that the word "horse" is actually not even a correct or compatible translation." There are attempts at translating the term for horse from Native languages into English such as "sacred dog," "elk dog" or "deer resembler," but "This is rather like trying to describe an eagle as a "hawk resembler" or a "sacred bird," as neither of these terms encompasses the holy reverence and symbolism with which the eagle is viewed by many Indigenous Nations." It is incredible to think that these creatures are too sacred and holy to be translated into a language like English, a language of erasure.

101. Running Horse Collin argues that the colonizers denied that indigenous people already had horses because owning horses was associated with power, nobility, and refinement, and they had to stick with the argument that indigenous people were uncivilized in order to justify colonizing them. I almost shout: and NOBODY bothered—or still bothers to correct this?! But I don't, because it's not a shock to anyone, is it?

102 Running Horse Collin includes several excerpts from interviews she conducted with horse caretakers, teachers, traditional knowledge bearers, ceremonial leaders/ medicine persons, scholars, and scientists. Here is one such excerpt: "One of the stories they talked about was the only thing that was more feared than the Natives was their horses. The people writing the notes said an Indian was killed, and they didn't say really 'Indian' but a Native was killed, a savage was killed, de-horsed, and the horse continued the attack without him. You know, carrying through our ranks and killing several of our men and several horses. And I thought that, and it was harder to kill the horse. The emphasis there was that it was more difficult to kill the horse. And there were several accounts of this. That the men in the attack were more afraid of the horses than they were of the warriors, or equally afraid of being attacked by the horses. And then, in one of the accounts that I did read from a Commander that he wrote back to the Command, that they were no longer able to proceed further north than they were at in the Colorado Territories. Of course, it wasn't listed as Colorado, but it was like "Trinidad," "Pueblo," and north of Pueblo, the established fort at Pueblo, because they

had no more horses ... And it wasn't the savages taking their horses, it was the stud horses coming into the camp at night and stealing the mares out, cutting them out and taking them. And killing their stud horses. They had to be real careful with their studhorses because if they didn't pen their stud horses up, corral them up and have security around them, these studs would come and kill them." Here is another excerpt: "I will tell you a story what my great-grandmother told me. I remember these stories because I was raised by 'the old ones' they call it in our language. And basically, my grandmother raised me. And my great-grandma they believe was born in 1880 and she died in 1976 when she was 96 years-old and she told us a lot of stories about everything. And right until the day she died she chopped her own wood. She carried her own water. She didn't want electricity or running water. She said that was not ... who we are. It wasn't "us." She was born before the first white man ever came to our settlements, our areas. And she told me a story about horses ... "Ponokomitta." "Ponokomitta" means "Elk Dog." That's how we translate it, horses. And she said, way back in the old days a man was leaving for the Oomspahtsikoo, the sand hills, to go and do a vision. When we do visions, we do it for four days and four nights with no food or water. And he walked and walked and walked and walked. And he came to this area that was almost uninhabited because there was no food or water anywhere. And I think we call it the Palace Triangle now in this territory. And after days beyond his quest, he got lost. He didn't know how to get back. So, he started seeing visions because he was dying. He was dying. No water, no food. And he seen this man riding this animal he's never seen in his life. He was chasing a buffalo. And that man speared that buffalo right in the neck and the buffalo dropped. And he went running over there over the bluff to say, 'Well, this man can save me. Hopefully he can feed me because I am dying.' When he got there, there was nothing there. But in the ground, he seen this mouse, with this spear grass stuck in his neck. And he goes, 'What the ... what am I seeing?' All of a sudden over the bluff there he seen these ears popping up, and it came over more and more. And there was this herd of Ponokomitta. And he was looking at them and they were looking at him. And this was the time when horses could talk to you. I don't mean how we talk with our mouth. But, through your minds. They walked up to him and they said, 'We know you are dying. We are going to help you. We are going to help you and your people. The only thing we say is you take care of us forever.

And you love us, and you love us divinely. And we will take care of you forever. And we will feed you and we will help you, clothe you and everything.' So, he got on the lead horse and that lead horse took him back to the camp because he was lost. And off this whole herd comes with him back to the camp. And when they came in, they seen this man that was gone for days and he brought in all these horses. That's how we got the horses. And we called them 'Ponokomitta,' ever since then, 'Elk Dogs.' So, that's the story she told me of how we got the horses. I like that story better than anything else and this story, I've tried to search for it. This story that was told to me has never been written, and she told that to me ... And so, we've always calmly known we've always had the horses. Way before the settlers came. The Spanish have never come through our area. So, there's no way they could have introduced that to us."

8.
I am Phantasmagoric

Don't Grab- Swallow Words

Sometimes, when I try to speak, I cannot think of words. Or I cannot string them together the way that language demands. Instead, I see clouds, ones I can look at but cannot grab. I want to show my listener the shape of the cloud, the texture, the color, but there are no words.

I suppose there are causes to the swallowing, the stifling, the far-away-ness of words for me:

The years spent boxed up in my mind without being able to speak.
The years spent being constantly corrected.
The years spent having an accent[103].
The years spent trying to say something but the thing coming out all wrong.
The years spent watching my mother fight rocks in her mouth.
The years spent miscommunicating with my own mother.
The years spent looking for validation.
The years spent needing a smile and a nod—an acknowledgment of understanding.
The years spent having to swallow the last of my words.

But here's the kicker: my listener is not stifling my words; I am. I am the one swallowing.

---

103. I didn't know that I had an accent when I first started speaking English until recently, when I watched a recording of myself from 5th grade. In the video I am on a cruise with classmates for our graduation trip, tracing the New York City skyline on a little boat on the Hudson. As part of the graduation video, they asked each student to share their favorite memory of P.S. 41. When I spoke, my English was coated in a thick Japanese accent. I shouldn't have been shocked—it had only been about a year since we moved to America, but I was shocked anyway. I didn't know I had an accent that I eventually got rid of. When did it go away? Where did it go?

Haiku Series

Often in Japan
I feel like a woman with
a parrot: subject

Of a gaze, never-
ending, never breaking, I
am an imposter.

Assuming gaze they
ask: what are you doing here?
Should I not be here?

Or instead the gaze
asks, Why did you ever leave?
I never asked to.

Who is the gazer?
What do they need to know? If
the parrot will speak?

No, it's not if the
parrot will speak—it's what lan-
guage it will speak in.

An Interaction at a コンビニ[104]

I walk into a コンビニ, the いらっしゃいませ![105] and cold air
rushing towards me, the sediments of familiarity settling on the
bottom of my stomach—*I have been here before. And before.* I
walk around the space, the aisles of potato chips in colorful bags
filled mostly with air, the fridges and freezers with microwavable
single meals, the ice creams I can taste on my tongue because
I tasted them again and again, sitting on the floor of my aunt's
house as a child. I pick something up—maybe a cold bottle of
green tea for my endless walking, or a salmon onigiri I want to
snack on, and I carry it over to the cashier, the ones that fake a
smile and happiness all day, probably exhausted inside but never
showing it, and I put the things I want to buy on the counter and I
say, お願いします[106] and all of a sudden the cashier looks at me in
shock, widens their eyes, flusters, and fights the rolling pebbles
in their mouth, trying to find the words to communicate with
me, to continue being the perfect cashier they were trained to be,
and they say something like, "Would you... bag? Chopsticks?"
in English and I answer, あ、大丈夫です。[107] in Japanese but they
hesitate for a long time, staring at the foreign in me, the white
in me, and their glance moves its way over to the machine, at
the amount of money I owe, trying to translate the numbers in
their mind, 650 yen, maybe, and I wait, feeling strange, feeling
unhelpful, feeling like an imposter, feeling alien, feeling like
maybe I am doing something I shouldn't, and I start looking
through my wallet for the money that I owe and at the same time
that I pull out my crisp 1,000-yen bill with the face of Hideyo
Noguchi on it, the bacteriologist who discovered the agent of
syphilis as the cause of paralytic disease, the erratic, volatile
researcher who conducted questionable human experiments at
the Rockefeller Institute in New York, I hear, "six...hundred-
and....fifty....yen.... please," and I nod, deeply, smile a little bit,
and say, ありがとうございます。[108]

104. Kombini: convenience store

105. Irasshaimase

106. Onegaishimasu

107. Ah, daijoubu desu

108. Arigatou gozaimasu

My Mother's Language

"Yo you sound mad monotonous when you talk to your mom on the phone," a friend teases me in the parking lot of Bay Terrace shopping center, our middle school stomping grounds. We'd taken a bus directly after school, passing our usual stops on the Q13, all the way down Bell Boulevard right before it turned to make its final stop at Bayside High School. I had just gotten off the phone with my mother to let her know I was there to catch a movie at AMC. わかってるわかってる！5時前には帰るから。[109] I told her before hanging up.

"Shut up! Really? This is just how I talk in Japanese," I say.

"You sound like a robot," somebody else in the group chimes in, making everyone laugh.

"I don't know why I do that!! You guys are so mean!!" I say, even though I secretly like the teasing, because it feels like an acceptance. An acceptance into a group of friends who all speak a language other than English at home. We all know we sound different when we speak our other language. We all think it's funny.

I am jealous of those who manage to keep speaking their home language all the way up to adulthood. In so many ways, I feel like a failure because at some point, I switched over to English, even though my mother still speaks Japanese to me. I mix Japanese words and phrases, but my grammar and most words are in English, because my speaking skills have deteriorated. Doesn't choosing English over my mother's language disappoint her? I know that it disappoints me.

The other day I told her about the first day of class this semester, about the students, what I taught, how it went, but a few days later she asked me, "When does class start again?" I wanted to snap at her for not listening, but maybe she didn't understand me when I told her about my first day. Sometimes, she makes me pause as I tell a story, asks for translations and definitions of unfamiliar words. And I always tell myself: *Just speak Japanese and you won't run into this problem.*

I've tried a few times in my adulthood to bring the Japanese back, to leave English on the shelf, but English is the language I had to cling onto to survive. My lifeline. How do I safely pry myself away? Each time I am pulled by English again and our conversations return to her speaking Japanese and me responding in English.

I want to keep fighting for Japanese, though. I don't want to give up. I want it to be like the way we first spoke to each other when I was young. I want her to not have to guess what her own daughter is saying. I want our conversations to reach deeper places. I want her to understand me. I want to feel safe speaking Japanese again.

---

109. I know, I know! I'll be home before 5.

unwanted role reversal

It is the day after seeing the movie at AMC in Bay Terrace. I came home a little later than I should've—the movie was long and the bus didn't come for a bit but I made sure to call my mother to let her know and she wasn't too angry when I came home past six. But I feel a little tinge of guilt, so when I hear her struggling on the phone, I slide over next to her on the couch and listen.

"Speak to a representative," she says, but the machine doesn't catch her L's for R's and she doesn't mush together the "entative" of "representative" like a native speaker would.

"If you'd like to hang up, please press the pound key," I hear a tiny voice from the inside the phone, and my mother lets out a deep sigh.

"Speak to a representative!" she tries again, louder. I mean, what else can she do other than raise her voice? It's not like she can suddenly change the way she speaks.

"Sorry, I didn't get that," the tiny voice says, mockingly.

"Speak… to… representative!!"

"If you'd like to hang up, please press the pound key."

Heat begins to rise from my gut, and I gesture for her to give me the phone. As though waiting for this moment, my mother quickly places the now-burning phone in my hand.

"Speak to a representative," I say, and the machine picks up my buttery American English immediately and the line to connect to a representative begins trilling.

I feel powerful. Like I have a key to a door that my mother does not have access to. Like she needs me. Like she relies on me. But now I think of how powerless she must have felt. Like an unwanted role reversal: my mother a babbling, wordless child and her 13-year-old daughter a language expert.

日本語は私の頭の中で生きている

One day in elementary school, a friend asked me,
"Why do you keep calling it パープル[110]? It's 紫色[111]。"

Japanese was my first language, but I'd learned some
words only in English. Like the way I've called my aunt ア
ンティ[112] all my life, or how I've never referred to spinach as
ほうれん草[113].

But now, it's the opposite, and Japanese creeps up a lot
when I am trying to speak English. I can't do multiplication
in English because I memorized the times table in Japanese.
Sometimes, I accidentally say, "You can go, the light's
blue" instead of green because in Japanese, we say 青[114]
instead of 緑[115] even though traffic lights in Japan are also
red, yellow, and green.

The first traffic signal in Japan was introduced in 1930,
on the crossroad of Hibiya, Tokyo. At first, drivers and
pedestrians did not know what each color symbolized, but
the reason Japanese people referred to the colors as "red,
yellow, and blue" is that in the Japanese language, blue
encompasses a wider range of colors than in English. For
example, green vegetables are referred to as 青野菜 or "blue
vegetables" and green leaves are referred to as 青葉な, or
"blue leaves." It also made sense to Japanese people for
the three traffic lights to be the three primary colors. So,
even though the word for green existed in Japanese, they
still called green light "blue light." I thought that was it, no
further research necessary, but then it was pointed out to me
recently, after I showed this writing to someone who has
spent some time in Japan, that the green light on a traffic
light in Japan is *actually* bluer—almost a turquoise color. I
immediately looked up traffic lights in Japan in comparison
to the U.S. on Google Images to confirm, and indeed the
signals in Japan have a bluish tint.

Initially, Japanese traffic lights were green, much like
the traffic lights in the U.S. However, the country's offi-

cial traffic documents still referred to green traffic lights as 青 because of the way the language includes shades of green as blue (as stated earlier). As time passed, though, 緑 became more widely used to refer to green, and so Japanese linguists began objecting their government's decision to continue using 青 to describe what was clearly 緑. In a way to compromise, the Japanese government "mandated through a cabinet order that traffic lights use the bluest shade of green possible—still technically green, but noticeably blue enough to justify continue using the 青 nomenclature." So, although the traffic lights in Japan look turquoise or almost completely blue, the government assures us it's actually just a very blue shade of green—green enough to satisfy international regulations, blue enough to still be called 青. Wild, that language had such an influence that it made even the government compromise. Who says language isn't power?

110. Paapuru

111. Murasaki iro: purple

112. Anti

113. Hōrensō

114. Ao: blue

115. Midori: green

リベッカ

Like I mentioned, the word "blue" encompasses shades of green in Japanese, and I learned that in Russian, there are different words for different shades of blue: light blue is "goluboy" and dark blue is "siniy." There's a Japanese word for "light blue" too: "水色[116]" which literally translates to "water color[117]."

My cousins' names are colors: 緑 Midori and 藍 Ai: Green and Indigo. They are not unusual Japanese names though typically, the kanji for Ai would be 愛, which means love. I suppose they wanted both children to be named after colors.

My name in Japanese is リベッカ[118] which is not a typical Japanese name at all.

One summer in second grade, I won a town-wide drawing contest. They held a small ceremony at the local library, and as we entered, they handed each of us a small booklet with the winners' names in it. I spotted my name and sat there proudly, waiting for them to call it so I could receive my certificate.

The girl who sat next to me looked a few grades older. She browsed through the booklet and paused on one of the pages. She whispered, "リベッカ. What the hell kind of name is that?"

She was just whispering to herself, and she didn't know that リベッカ was actually sitting right next to her, but I was shocked. If I were brave and courageous, I would've turned to her and said, "Do you have a problem with my name?" but I stayed quiet. I wanted to hide, and I kept begging over and over in my mind, "Please don't call out my name." I didn't even care about the certificate anymore.

Eventually, they called out 鈴木リベッカ and I had to stand up, walk to the front, and receive my award. My mom, who was standing in the back smiled and waved to me, but I looked away. I was ashamed and angry at her for giving me such a stupid name. Why couldn't she name me after a color like my cousins?

I don't remember what happened when I went to sit back down next to the girl who'd insulted my name. Maybe she looked at me with a mortified expression, apologetic and regretful about her comment, or maybe she just ignored me. I know that she didn't say anything to me.

リベッカ/りべっか/Ribekka/
レベッカ/Rebecca

What the hell kind of name is that?

---

116. Mizu iro

117. There is also 肌色 (hada iro) or "skin color" which I wanted to mention. I remember seeing 肌色 in my colored pencil and crayon boxes and using them to color in people's skin. According to Wikipedia, the color is a light orange meant to match the skin color of an average Japanese person of the Mongoloid race. It is officially categorized in the JIS or Japan Industrial Standards (along with 268 other colors). I was kind of horrified reading all of this, but scrolled to a section titled, "Efforts to Combat Racial Discrimination" under which it says that most stationary makers renamed the color in 2000, and an official ban took place in 2005-6. Crayola banned its "flesh color" crayon in the U.S. in 1962.

118. Ribekka. Typically, Rebecca is written out as レベッカ (Rebekka) but my mother wanted the first letter of my name to match the first letter of her name (which is りえ[Rie]) in Japanese, so she changed it to リベッカ. This caused me to mispronounce my own name when I first moved to America.

when I didn't know how to say my own name anymore

I was paralyzed by fear during the first few weeks of school in America. English buzzed in my ears and stung me all over, forming painful welts on my skin. I never knew what was going on around me. I woke up every morning with a stomachache which settled at the pit like a heavy stone. Maybe that's the reason I always felt like I was carrying more than my body.

One day, I followed my classmates down the hall to the library to make library cards. When we sat down in the room, the library teacher, an older woman with stern eyes and short red hair came around to jot down our names for our cards.

"What's your name?" she asked when she came around to me.

"リベッカ" I whispered.

"Say it again?"

"リベッカ," I tried a little louder.

"How do you spell that?"

"リベッカ"

"No, I'm asking you how it's spelled."

"リベッカ"

"How do you *spell* it?! I'm asking you how to *spell* your name…"

Finally, a boy sitting at my table answered for me. "Her name is Rebecca. R-e-b-e-c-c-a."

"*Thank* you."

Life is filled with moments you're supposed to forget but don't.

on listening to your brain

To a prompt for a paper about language and identity, a student asks me:

"Professor, what if I don't know which language the voice within is speaking?" she tells me: "My father spoke Tajik, my mother Uzbek, but because I grew up in the Soviet Union and they put so many countries together, in primary school I often didn't understand what my friends were saying. Then I was told to only speak Russian and forget my native languages, so Russian became my main language, but now I'm here and I am using English."

I ask her: "Do you mix all of those languages when you think or speak?"

"Yes yes, and I want to teach my children how to speak them too."

"Do you believe that language and identity are directly connected? Do you feel like because you have access to so many languages that you can separate your identity from your languages?"

"I do think language and identity are connected. I just don't know how."

I am not helpful.
I'm not able to offer her advice, just my wandering thoughts and more questions to consider.

Now I think: she is phantasmagoric. What? I remember that a writer called a weasel phantasmagoric. So is she a weasel then? I can't tell her that, she'd probably get confused. Or worse, angry. She might think: I am not an exhibition of optical effects and illusions. I am not a constantly shifting complex succession of things seen or imagined. I am not a scene that constantly changes. I am not a bizarre or fantastic combination, collection, or assemblage. I am also not a carnivorous mammal that is able to prey on animals larger than themselves, are mostly brown with white or yellowish underparts, and in northern forms turn white in winter, or a light self-propelled tracked vehicle built either for traveling over snow, ice, or sand or as an amphibious vehicle, or a sneaky, untrustworthy, or insincere person.

I learn from a theory called translanguaging that we have always conceptualized languages as being in boxes. Each language a separate entity. English in one box; Japanese in another. But that this way of thinking is harmful and inaccurate. I don't have neat boxes in my brain. Neither does my student. Nobody does. The box idea comes from turning concepts into objects. So that we as humans can understand things that are very abstract: by boxing them in as objects. But there's also a history of power and violence behind the creation of said boxes. One box is superior to another. One box is more preferred than another. One box gets you further in society than another. One box can get you killed.

So, I was wrong in asking my student if multiple languages got in the way of finding a single identity. I was projecting. I believed in the box theory; she never did. She listened to her brain; I didn't.

Even if the voice inside your head is speaking in a hundred languages, you are still a single entity. You have a single identity. There aren't a hundred boxes in your brain—just one Language.

I am Phantasmagoric[119]

頭の中には一つの language[120] だけなんだって。[121]日本語でかんがえ
ても英語でかんがえてもリベッカはリベッカなんだって。[122] でも名前ま
で変わっちゃうのに本当に一緒の人なのかなあ？[123] Like, I do feel
slightly different.[124] Which kind of sucks because I really love
the idea of having just one language in your brain.[125] 日本語をは
なす自分はどこにいってしまったのだろう、ってよく[126] I question it,
staring out into the distance like some ancient philosopher,[127] で
もまだいるじゃん！ちゃんと[128] I just need to pay closer attention.[129]
Listen more. Take my own advice, because I'm always saying
shit like, "People just need to listen more.[130]" Um, hello,[131] それ
は自分もでしょ。[132] 日本語で一生懸命しゃべろうとしている Rebecca
も聞いてあげなさい。[133] 英語みたいにすぐには出てこないかもしれな
いけど[134] you need to be patient.[135] Give her time and space.[136] が
んばろ。[137]

---

120. 私は変幻自在

121. Apparently, we all only have one language.

122. Whether I think in Japanese or in English, I am still Rebecca.

123. But even my name shifts in each language, so am I really the same
person?

124. やっぱりちょっと違う感じがするんだけどなあ。

125. 頭の中には言葉が一つっていう考えがすごく好きだからこの気持ちをど
うすればいいのかなあ。

126. Where did the me that speaks in Japanese go?! I often

127. きくの、窓を見つめながら、大昔のフィロソフィーみたいにね

128. But she's here, still!

129. もっと目を留めないと。

130. もっと聞き入らないと。

131. 自分のアドバイスを受け入れないと。いつも「人はもっと聞き入れないとダメ」とか言ってるじゃん！おーい

132. I need to do this myself…

133. Please also listen carefully to the Rebecca that is trying really hard to speak in Japanese.

134. It may take her longer than in English but

135. ちょっと待っててあげて。

136. 時間とスペースあげて。

137. Let's do this

9.
She Will Only Shine Bright

Moon Song

There is a song in 文部省唱歌[118] called つき[119].

Here are the lyrics:

でた　　でた　　つきが
deta　　*deta*　　*tsukiga*
out　　out　　the moon

まるい　まるい
marui　*marui*
round　round

まんまるい
manmarui
perfectly round

ぼんのような
bon no youna
tray-　like

つきが
tsukiga
the moon

かくれた　　　くもに
kakureta　　*kumoni*
hid　　　behind cloud

くろい　くろい
kuroi　*kuroi*
black　black

まっくろい
makkuroi
pitch black

すみのような
sumi no youna
like ink

くもに
kumo ni
the cloud

また　　でた　　つきが
mata　deta　tsukiga
again　out　the moon

まるい　まるい
marui　marui
round　　round

まんまるい
manmarui
perfectly round

ぼんのような
bon no youna
tray- like

つきが
tsukiga
moon

---

138. Monbushou shouka: songs selected by the Ministry of Education
to be taught in school from 1910 until 1944. I'd never heard of
it, so I decided to look up some songs on YouTube. The songs
sound like a church choir, and the lyrics are incredibly poetic.
I was also intrigued by the comments on the videos. They were
filled with nostalgia: some saying the song would be played in
their hometown every morning at 6 am; some remembering dead
grandparents who would play or sing the songs; some mourning
the extinction of birds and animals that used to live in the area
mentioned in the song. It seems these songs are deeply rooted in
Japanese history and culture, and to listen to these songs is to be
Japanese.

139. Tsuki: moon. The song was written in 1911. A link to a recording
of an elementary school chorus singing it in 1959 is here: https://
www.youtube.com/watch?v=k2Q6Qe7DrxE.

untitled

Tanka:

Just because the moon is behind clouds doesn't mean she stopped shining

Tanka 2:

Just because you stopped shining doesn't mean you don't count

A sentence in Japanese:

おぼんのようなおつきさまはわたしたちのことをみまもっているわけで
はない
Tray-   like   moon   us   watching over
not

A Haibun about Different Sides of the Moon

When we still lived in Japan, my mother would say that the moon looked different in Japan than it did in the U.S. and I believed her.

"See in Japan, there's a rabbit inside of the moon doing 餅つき[140]. In America, they say there's a crab dancing on the surface. Or a witch. We must be looking at different sides of the moon."

I only learned that the moon looks the same whether you're in Japan or in the U.S. when I got older[141]. We must have just arrived at different interpretations of what the surface of the moon looks like. I mean of course, 餅つき is very specifically Japanese.

The moon is the moon, and it has been the moon for as long as we've been living on this planet. It's one of the only constant things in our lives. I wonder if that's the reason we obsess over it, even though おつきさまはわたしたちのことをみまもっているわけではない.

My mother and I have a conversation about the neighbors we had in Japan. Most of them we knew well, because I went to school with the kids in the neighborhood, and the parents would often get together and talk.

"今は何やってるんだろうね?[142]"

"全然分かんない[143]。But looks like most of them stayed in 知多市."

知多市, or Chita-city, is a small town in Aichi prefecture about a 30-minute train ride from Nagoya, the third largest city in Japan. It was a pretty obscure town until a major international airport (Chubu Centrair International Airport) was built in the nearby Tokoname City. Building for the airport began in August 2000, which is 8 months before I left for New York. Locals were initially upset about its construction, particularly because fishermen were paid out of their jobs to stop fishing in the waters around the airport; the annual summer fireworks festival at Shinmaiko Beach had to be cancelled indefinitely; and those whose houses would interrupt the new trainline to the airport were paid a sum to abandon their homes. Despite this initial reaction, the locals seem to now favor the airport: it gives people job opportunities (my cousin works at a shop in the airport), there is more tourism around the area, and real estate seems to have gone up.

In the twenty years we've been absent, I wonder how else the neighborhood has evolved. I'll bet many of my old classmates are married with children by now. I'll bet their kids are going to the same elementary school we went to. I wonder what their days looked like since the day I left.

Look to the moon for answers
but she will only
shine bright

---

140. Mochitsuki: mochi pounding

141. Though of course, the moon does indeed look different if you go to the Southern Hemisphere. It would appear "upside down." https://moon.nasa.gov/about/top-moon-questions/#:~:text=A%3A%20 No%2C%20everyone%20sees%20the,you're%20used%20to!)

142. I wonder what they're up to now

143. I have no idea

The Moon is Just the Moon

I often played pretend as a kid but I wonder if we stop playing pretend when we grow up because that's all we do when we grow up. We stop pretending to be interesting things like okra, and pretend to be: office worker, subway rider, coffee drinker, American, Japanese. Playing pretend all the time makes us lose sight of ourselves. I often wonder if the child that I once was is my true self. And I wonder how I can get that back. Can I get it back? Is that why I feel so sad when I think about childhood, because it's the true me that I'll never have again?

I can't describe who I am using words, but I am trying to describe who I am using words. What would childhood me say about that? "That's stupid." Humans have tried to figure out what defines us: our past experiences; our cultures; our languages; our family and ancestors; our careers; our children; our religious beliefs; our education; etc.; a combination of it all. But what are we when all of that is stripped? Nothing?

The moon doesn't have this problem though, does it?

on naming, marking, erasing

I decide to look up how to say moon in every language. I'm sure some languages are missing[144] on this list, but here is a list:

月/moon/ hënë/ilargia/ месяц/mjesec/ луна/lluna/luna/Luna/ měsíc/ mane/maan/Kuu/kuu/lune/moanne/ lúa/ φεγγάρι/ hold/Tungl/ mēness/ mėnulis/Mound/ месечината/qamar/ måne/ księżyc/lua/ lună/ ghealach/ месец/mesiac/ ай/ місяць/lleuad/ ענאָוועל/լուսին/ay/চাঁদ/月亮/მთვარე/ચંદ્ર/चांद/ hli /ಚಂದ್ರನ /ព្រះច័ន្ទ/달/ ເດືອນ /ചന്ദ്രൻ /cap/လ/ चन्द्र / ଜହ /سپوږمۍ/ ਚੰਦ / چنڊ /සඳ /мох/ சந்திரன் / చంద్రుడు / ดวงจันทร์/ Aý/ئاي /چاند/oy /mặt trăng /ירח /hêv/ماه /maan/mwezi/ ጨረቃ/watã/ọnwa/ukwezi/khoeli/mwedzi/inyanga/oṣupa/bulan/ buwan/mahina/rembulan/volana/marama/masina/luno/lalin

Is księżyc different from Луна is different from 달 from месечината is different from hënë is different from 月? If they're all different, what is that bright object in the night sky? If they're all the same, why does it have so many different names? By naming the moon, are we not actually just naming ourselves?

---

144. Many languages are erased/ forgotten or are in the process of being erased/ forgotten. For example, this list does not include *killa*, which is moon in Quechua, an indigenous language spoken by the Quechua peoples, primarily living in the Peruvian Andes. It also does not include チュプ (chupu), which is moon in the language spoken by the Ainu people, an East Asian ethnic group indigenous to Japan, the original inhabitants of Hokkaidō. The "near-total assimilation of the Ainu into Japanese society has resulted in many individuals of Ainu descent having no knowledge of their ancestry." https://archive.org/details/ainuofjapan00pois/page/4/mode/2up. Several days after writing this, I came across Mirene

Arsanios' Notes on Mother Tongues in which she writes, "Native languages, like other endangered species, are going extinct. On January 4, 1984, for example, the last speaker of Yavitero—an Arawakan language spoken near the Atabapo river in Venezuela—died together with the last Yavitero words" (2).

When I printed out this page at Staples, I noticed that many of the scripts did not print. They turned into empty boxes, as seen in photo below. Language being erased.

月/moon/ hënë/ilargia/ месяц/mjesec/ луна/lluna/luna/Luna/mjesec/ mĕsíc/ mane/maan/Kuu/kuu/lune/moanne/ lúa/ φεγγάρι/hold/Tungl/ mēness/ ménulis/Mound/ месечината/qamar/ måne/ księżyc/lua/ lună/ Луна/ghealach/ месцц/mesiac/ ай/мiсяць/lleuad/ עֶוואָנצ/לעוואָנצ/ʃnιuħŭ/ay/□□□□/月亮/θ σχ ɔ ६ŋ /□□□□□/□□□□/hli/□ᑌᑌ□□□□/ай/[ʃ: ɢʂ/달/□□□□□/□□□ᑌ□□□/□□□□□/cap/∞/ □□□□□□/□□ᑌᑌ□□/ سم پوزرمی / □□□/ ۱ا/ قمر چ نڋ/᠖᠖ʤmox/□□□□□□□/□□□□□□□□/ดวงจันทร์/Aÿ/ ي چاد د/چاي نؤoy/māt trăng/ ᠋ חרי/hêv/

ماہ/maan/mwezi/□□□/watã/ọnwa/ukwezi/khoeli/mwedzi/inyanga/oṣupa/bulan/buwan/mahina/rembulan/volana/marama/masina/luno/lalin

A Haibun About Moon, My Mother, and Me

She and I: the moon and Rebecca: 月とリベッカ: we stare at
each other across the 238,855 miles in between us. (Did you
know that the moon is getting further away from the earth each
year? What should we make of that?) Her glow leaking into the
Hudson River below, I run out to the balcony of my apartment
to see her without the glass window between us. The nighttime
air tries to swallow me into its darkness, wrapping me up slowly
from all sides, but I stand firm, my feet planted on the floor. I
look at her even though I know she cannot see me, and I whisper,
Thank you. Thanking the moon is something I've inherited—
whenever my mother sees her shining like a silver coin in the
sky, she claps her hands twice, then puts her palms together in
front of her, bows, and closes her eyes to say a little prayer: ナン
マンダブ。今日もありがとう。So, like my mother, I thank the moon
for being the lone shining guide in a dark sea and for being so
beautiful and for pulling and pushing the tide and for coming
back again. But more than that, maybe, for shifting shape. For
being the piece of the nail after it's been clipped, a half-eaten
pizza pie, a seashell, a slice of orange, a croissant, a shrimp, a
dumpling. But still being the moon. Because I too, am so many
things but still me. I am constantly shifting shapes, being called
hundreds of different names in all languages.

お月様ありがとう。*Thank you, moon.*

After releasing a sigh, I go back inside, enter the warmth of my
apartment again, rejoice in the beauty I've just witnessed, and
think to myself: *as long as the moon is here, I will not disappear.*

And I walk over to the kitchen where my mother is standing by
the sink, gently washing rice with her fingertips, the rice she
scooped out of the huge bag of California grains we bought and
carried from Mitsuwa, the Japanese grocery store we moved to
be closer to. When I tell her about the moon she pauses briefly,
looks into my eyes, and smiles. "みたよ。きれいだね。" she tells

me. She is here. I am here. We are both here—here, anywhere.
Under the moon.

She sees in the moon
a spot in the sky proving
our existence marked

Acknowledgments

Thank you to all the Asian American writers and artists who came before me, for paving the way and giving me courage to write in the way I want to write; to say the things I want to say.

Thank you to everyone who guided me in getting this book to where it needed to be. For being readers that I treasure and for our conversations about the moon and ginkgo trees: Katie Machen, Francesca Hyatt, Marco Navarro, Cynthia Rivera, Jay Boss Rubin, Nora Carr, Eleanor Whitney, Kiyo Kamisawa, L Torres, Daniella DiMaggio, Roger Sedarat, and Annmarie Drury.

Thank you, Natalia Stypulkowski, Rachel Rosengard, Sanne Lynam, Jennifer Kang, Kanami Asaoka, and Kaori Onogi for being friends so close to my heart, for believing in me all this time.

Thank you, Ryan Fark, for your friendship and for painting the gorgeous cover.

Thank you, Hanging Loose Press and especially my editor Caroline Hagood for believing in my work and allowing me to move forward even when it initially faced challenges.

Thank you, Judith Suzuki for being born. Life made so much more sense after you came into the world. I am so lucky to call myself your sister.

Thank you to my late father for telling my mother, "Our daughter is a storyteller" and recognizing the writer in me when I was just a little girl. I am just like you.

And of course, thank you to my mother. It is impossible to express how much love I have for you. Without you, I would not be. You are an incredible woman.